PASTORAL CARE
TO BLACK SOUTH AFRICANS

American Academy of Religion
Academy Series

edited by
Susan Thistlethwaite

Number 67
PASTORAL CARE
TO BLACK SOUTH AFRICANS

by
Howard H. Eybers

Howard H. Eybers

PASTORAL CARE
TO BLACK SOUTH AFRICANS

Scholars Press
Atlanta, Georgia

PASTORAL CARE
TO BLACK SOUTH AFRICANS

by
Howard H. Eybers

© 1991
The American Academy of Religion

Library of Congress Cataloging in Publication Data

Eybers, Howard H. (Howard Henry)
    Pastoral care to black South Africans / Howard H. Eybers.
    p. cm. — (American Academy of Religion academy series ; no.
67)
    Includes bibliographical references.
    ISBN 1-55540-401-4 — ISBN 1-55540-402-2
    1. Blacks—Pastoral counseling of—South Africa. I. Title.
II. Series.
BV4468.2.B55E92   1990
259'.089'968—dc20   90-25465
                                                     CIP

Printed in the United States of America
on acid-free paper

To the memory of
my father and mother
Jacobus and Kathleen Eybers,
the two most responsible
and generative people
I have ever known

TABLE OF CONTENTS

INTRODUCTION 1
    Focus of Book 1
    Theological 3
    Psychological 4
    Choice of Psychologist 12
    Choice of Ethicist 13
    Method 17

Chapter
1. ERIKSON'S LIFE CYCLE THEORY 21
    The Stages 23
    Freud 34
    William James 35
    Modes of Generativity 44
    Virtues 45
    Epigenesis 51
    Discussion Between Wright and Browning ... 52

2. NIEBUHR'S ETHICS OF RESPONSIBILITY ... 55
    The Structure of Niebuhr's Theology 55
    The Meaning of Responsibility 58
    The Symbol of Responsibility 60
    The Self in the Conceptual Scheme of
      Responsibility 64
    The Concept of Radical Monotheism 76
    Jesus as our Model of Responsibility 78
    Some Critique of Niebuhr's Ethics 81
    Christian Story/Human Story 83

3. AN ETHICAL-PSYCHOLOGICAL MODEL 87
    Responsibility and Generativity 95
    The Self as a Connecting Point Between
      Ethics and Psychology 115
    Erikson's Ideas About the Self 115
    Niebuhr's Ideas About the Self 116
    Significance of Trust in Erikson's Theory and
      Niebuhr's Ethics 120

4. THE STORIES OF FIVE ADULTS 123
   Case Studies 123
   Ethical-Psychological Interpretations 150
   General Summary of the Five Cases 179

5. IMPLICATIONS FOR PASTORAL CARE IN
   SOUTH AFRICA 185
   The Image of the Living Human Document . 187
   Gadamer's Idea of the Fusion of Horizon . . . 193
   Life Cycle Theory and Pastoral Care
   (Capps) 196
   The Moral Context of Pastoral Care 206

NOTES 213

REFERENCES 229

PREFACE

To love and to care for their children and to be responsive and responsible to them is the wish of every parent. Black South African parents are no exception. However these processes are complicated by dynamics in that society. Furthermore, their range for ethical action is severely curtailed by a racist government who upholds an immoral policy called apartheid. Thus, contrary to their God-given parental inclinations, black South African adults are prevented from being fully responsible/ responsive and fully generative to their children due to the limitations that are imposed upon them by an immoral society. Many of them have refused to allow the laws of South Africa to force them into a state of irresponsibility/ unresponsiveness and stagnation. For this they and their children have suffered. Many have lost their lives.

Many South African pastors execute pastoral care on a superficial basis due to fear of offending the authorities. Thus they are oblivious to the deeper needs of their people, e.g., moral, psychological, and political. The black youth of South Africa observe this and resent it. Thus, they come into conflict with such pastors and adults whom they accuse of being docile and complacent. The result is alienation from parents and church as well as identity confusion. The life and witness of the church also suffer in the process.

This book is an attempt to address the above problem. I do not claim to have all the answers, neither do I wish to convey the impression that all pastors and black adults are guilty of the above. On the whole, they are a courageous people. Even if some of these individuals are guilty, I sympathize with them. They are in a difficult situation. With this book I hope to make a small contribution towards the alleviation of the problem in question. My most original contribution in this book is what I refer to as an Ethical-Psychological Model. I present this model to black adults and pastors as an instrument of analysis for the lives that are enmeshed in the ethical and psychological problems under discussion. I trust that my model would enable the people who are the focus of this book to gain deeper insight and understanding of the ethical and psychological dimensions of the problems that they are experiencing. My ultimate hope and prayer is that they would be enabled by God through his shepherds to find a way to greater responsibility/responsiveness and generativity in their lives.

I need to thank a number of people without whose care, love, guidance, and support I would never have been able to complete this book. First, I want to give thanks to God for his grace and mercy throughout this arduous process. My wife Rosetta and our children Oscar, Heather, and Stacey-Anne have been my constant and greatest sources of inspiration and encouragement. My deepest appreciation goes to several faculty members of Princeton Theological Seminary, particularly Drs. Capps, Lapsley, and Livezey for their guidance and encouragement, as well as to Robina Leeper for typing the manuscript.

May the Lord use this book in such a way that it might enable everyone who reads it, through His Spirit, to become more responsible, responsive, and generative day by day. In this way we could make this world a better place for all of us to live in, particularly our children and those of future generations.

Howard Henry Eybers
Princeton, New Jersey
April 9, 1989

INTRODUCTION

Focus of Book

This book focuses on Responsibility and Generativity in the context of the inability of many black adults in South Africa to exercise it fully due to the fact that their range for ethical action is limited in that country. Responsibility in this regard refers to the black adult who has gained a sense of identity, intimacy, and generativity. By generativity is meant a sense of care and responsibility for the next generation. This problem gives rise to the following difficulties that black youth experience, namely a struggle to assimilate a radical monotheistic faith in the one universal God and great difficulty in achieving a clear positive identity.

Most black adults in South Africa experience despair, hopelessness, and confusion as a result of their inability to reach their youth, particularly in the present crisis situation. Aggression, resentment, and alienation from parents and society seem to be increasing. This intergenerational problem is not only common to black adults in South Africa. But for the purposes of this book I have chosen to focus on them due to a common bond that we share. Furthermore my self-understanding evolved out of the matrix of black adult-youth relationships. I want to suggest that the problem in question goes beyond the common intergenerational conflicts encountered in any normal parent-child relationship. The reason for this is that South African society as well as the tyrannical relationship that exists between the dominant white group in South Africa and blacks contribute toward this. Many black adults are currently experiencing a sense of having lost control.

The dilemma that faces these adults is moral and psychological in character. Thus, in order to find a solution it has to be approached from these perspectives. Other problems that have come to the fore in this stagnant environment are: alienation of black youth from the

Christian Church, a faith crisis, injury to the black self, low self esteem, meaninglessness, self-absorption (on the part of parents), as well as irresponsibility and unresponsiveness.

These problems but more specifically stagnation and irresponsibility on the part of black parents have to be addressed by parents and particularly pastoral care givers. The increasing alienation of black youth from the church as well as the critical position of parent-child relationships suggest that the pastoral care methods of black pastors as well as many white pastors serving black congregations are inadequate and impoverished. These methods could be characterized as "quick fixes" and biblicistic in most cases. The superficial nature of these methods furthermore arises due to the fact that these pastors neglect to examine and analyze the political, cultural, and psychosocial dynamics that impinge upon the psyches of black people.

There are reasons for this inadequacy and impoverishment. Black pastors are aware of the political, economical, and cultural matrix of the pastoral problems confronting their flocks. But, many of them are afraid of drawing politics into the solution. In doing so they would risk imprisonment or other forms of harassment by the police. It could also lead to the alienation of members from the church who hold conservative points of view, particularly on a political level. Many black pastors have chosen to be faithful to the Gospel of Jesus Christ and to their Lord in the execution of their pastoral care duties. Ordinarily this amounts to the criticizing of unjust political structures that impinge upon the human rights and dignity of God's people. For such pastors the consequences have been painful and punitive.

White pastors serving black congregations in South Africa, particularly in rural areas, usually portray paternalistic and nationalistic traits. There is evidence that most of them first and foremost pledge their allegiance to their government, which has made itself guilty of violating the moral existence of black people with their apartheid policies, instead of to God. This attitude has removed their ability to approach the problems of their black parishioners from a holistic perspective as it would mean placing the blame of a very large portion of the plight of these people on their government. Ultimately this has led to an impoverished and halfhearted way of doing pastoral care. It is this kind of irrelevant or partially adequate form of pastoral care giving that this book seeks to address. In this regard Don Browning's thoughts on the moral context of pastoral care are most helpful. The much needed holistic approach to pastoral care is eliminated and problems of irresponsibility and stagnation persist.

Due to feelings of inadequacy on a pastoral level many black pastors make themselves guilty of executing conflicting pastoral care approaches. In many cases this is due to desperation to render comfort and sustenance. The result is that black Christians begin to view the church to which they turn as the last hope for comfort, hope, and answers to their moral, psychological, and spiritual problems as a failure. This failure is not intentional of course but it signals the fact that pastoral care givers need to find new instruments of analysis for the problems of those who are experiencing an imbalance in the human condition. I want to suggest that one of the main reasons for their failure is due to the fact that pastors have neglected to incorporate the insights of disciplines like psychology, sociology, and theological subdisciplines like ethics.

Theological

From a theological perspective black adults in South Africa could be viewed as experiencing a deep yearning for a pastoral care and a love that will open up God's hope, healing, and saving power and illuminating revelation to them--a revelation of the One who could create order out of their psychological and morally chaotic situation. Niebuhr speaks about revelation as follows: "Revelation means for us that part of our inner history which illuminates the rest of it and which is itself intelligible." That part of our inner history is Jesus. Through Him we are enabled to understand all other events.[1] Niebuhr is thus saying that by means of revelation we are enabled to make sense out of the confusion (in this case stagnation and unresponsiveness and irresponsibility) that surrounds and affects us and we are given a sense of worth, value, generativity, and responsibility.

Psychological

From a psychological perspective black adults find it hard to accept that they are ungenerative towards their youth and that they have failed in their role as parents to a certain degree. There is also the lack or absence of an adequate hermeneutical instrument to interpret their moral and psychological dilemma to their children as well as to bring about deeper self-comprehension. Coupled to this is the fact that it is very painful to engage in self-analysis. This has given rise to the problem of an ongoing psychological and moral process over generations, a process that has greatly contributed to stagnation and irresponsibility. Much of the blame for this ungenerativity and irresponsibility is oftentimes instinctively placed on the shoulders of the dominant group and the government of South Africa. While these two groups should share a large part of the blame and while there is a lot of justification for this rationale it proves to be unproductive in the long run. This does not contribute any solution to the problem but serves to entrench it in ethically and morally stagnant behavior. It is like consuming aspirin when surgery is needed. Black South Africans are desperate to find any kind of relief from their dilemma, a dilemma that has kept alive a state of irresponsibility and ungenerativity over generations. This process must be disrupted in order to foster mental and spiritual growth.

One of the positive ways of going about matters to achieve the latter is for black adults to be enabled by means of the ethical-psychological model to perceive how they have yielded too much power to the forces in their country that constitute the genesis point of irresponsibility and generativity. In this way they may be enabled to understand that the latter need not be feared as powers that are too great to conquer and to oppose. When these forces are placed in a relationship with God as the Center of Value, their power and character of invincibility decrease. Niebuhr contributes a valuable point in this regard. He says:

> To the monotheistic believer for whom all responses to his companions are interrelated with his responses to God as the ultimate person, the ultimate cause, the center of universal community, there seem to be indications in the whole of the responsive accountable life of men of a movement of self-judgment and self-guidance which cannot come to rest until it makes its reference to a universal other and a universal community which that other both represents and makes its cause. . . . I only register this observation, that these social theories of the moral life as responsible are neither just to the empirical facts nor consistent with their fundamental ideal if they stop such analysis at the point of reference to the ethos, or the judging actions of a closed society to which man responds in all his responses to his companions.[2]

Niebuhr's point suggests to the South African situation that Black Adults should use God and him alone as their REFERENCE POINT. Such a relational existence with God as reference point will empower black adults and all

Christians for that matter to respond to all actions on them with responsibility and generativity because they will see that in times of crisis when they ask about "the ultimate causes and the ultimate judges"[3] that "our life in response to actions upon us, our life in anticipation of response to our reactions, takes place within a society whose boundaries cannot be drawn in space, or time, or extent of interaction, short of a whole in which we live and move and have our being."[4]

While black adults struggle with the psychological and moral/ethical problems in question the erosion of adult-child relationships continues and resignation, despair, rage, violence, and identity confusion continue. In the process many young people are alienated from God and his church. Juvenile crime is increasing in alarming proportions in South Africa. This must, beyond a shadow of doubt, have a connection with the collapsing of formerly strong family systems and parent-child relationships that were strongly based on Christian values and respect mutually. Due to their disillusionment with the church and the authorities many young people are turning toward marxism. In this regard I refer the readers to the story of Mr. A. in chapter 4 of this book. His is a classical example of this dilemma. This ideology spells a critical situation for intergenerational relationships among black South Africans and for the Christian Church and its pastoral care role in that country.

However, this moral-psychological crossroad should be viewed by black South African pastors not with total despair but as an opportunity to exercise relevant, meaningful, and holistic pastoral care. This should be a pastoral care that implements methods which take cognizance of the insights revealed by psychology, specifically personality theorists like Erikson and ethicists like H. Richard Niebuhr. This could render a valuable contribution towards narrowing the hiatus in parent-child relationships created by the stagnant context under discussion. I believe that my ethical-psychological model will play an important role in this regard. It is a model that rejects a superficial analysis of the problems of black South African adults that does not take into consideration the deeper, underlying psychological and moral-ethical dimensions of their problems. The latter are also linked to socio-political-economical factors in their sphere of existence. This model affirms the identities of these adults in the face of environmental forces that reinforce identity confusion. This model also affirms the potential of these people to be fully generative and responsible. Furthermore it will contribute to the growth, integration, and health of the black family in South Africa particularly as far as child-parent relationships are concerned. This in turn will lead to a more relevant comprehension of the Gospel of Jesus Christ and the pastoral care and pastoral theology that is firmly rooted in that Gospel. Ultimately, I have the vision and firm belief that my model can contribute to an increase in faith on the part of black Christians in South Africa in him who is their Center of Value and the One who invites them to place their fidelity and commitment in him. He is the one who alone can empower them to have a SELFHOOD grounded in him and who can empower them to be generative and responsible. On the psychological side Erikson's theory can enable the black pastor to understand generativity and stagnation better as well as the way that the human personality develops. This would help them in their walk and sustenance-giving of their troubled parishioners as they support them in their pain and despair. It could also aid them to detect the danger signals in the life cycles of those to whom they render pastoral care as well as those whose lives are in a "cogwheeling relationship" with theirs before the crises that crop up at various life stages spin out of control.

With the aid of our model black parents could also be assisted to interpret the behavior of their youth towards them in a realistic fashion. Erikson's theory could aid them to understand the identity confusion of their youth as it evolves from an epigenetic base in a cogwheeling relationship with their personalities. Psychologically many black adults have to be helped to face the fact that they need to undergo the painful process of restructuring their self-concepts and to drop some of the masks that they have worn as a kind of defense mechanism/survival mechanism against the racist onslaughts of a closed and oppressive society. By acting in such a way they have not existed as the people of God with a sense of God-given self-worth and value that he wants them to be. This is due to the fact that they have responded to forces that have negated their existence and not to the One who helps to transcend this negation. Faith in God is of the essence in such a situation. Once again our model could be relevant in bringing it about. Our model brings together, at points common to theology, ethics and psychology perspectives that could be employed by pastoral care givers to restructure distorted personalities. One such common point is identity which we have correlated with faith in chapter three. Loder's thoughts on the recentering of the personality put the struggle of the negated, shamed, and injured black self in a balanced perspective in his book *The Transforming Moment*.[5] He says, in talking about Luther, that his longing to look God in the face was not merely a desire for the expulsion of guilt and shame but for a fundamental recentering of his personality on a face that would never leave him.[6] In this regard Loder is referring to a reality that has a transcendental character around which the personality of the black adult and every adult irrespective of color should be centered. Loder's thought enables me to put the damaged ego of black adults in a healing and divine perspective. He says that this damaged ego that is "searching for God" does have HOPE of healing and restoration because "decentering the ego liberates and empowers its functioning even though, and precisely because, it is no longer the presumed center of the personality."[7]

There is evidence that many black pastors in South Africa exhibit acute limitations on the level of the integration of psychology, theology and ethics. This has an impoverishing effect on the method and nature of the kind of pastoral care of individuals who are recipients thereof. This deficiency gives rise to the following question, namely: How can ministers and pastoral care givers exercise more effective and relevant pastoral care to black adults in particular without engaging the insights of disciplines like psychology and sociology and ethics. The answer is: It cannot be done. If it is done in this manner it will prove to be deficient. In this book I will indicate that pastoral care can be done with the aid of pastoral theology and psychology and still preserve the integrity of both disciplines.

With the integrated approach pastoral care givers would be enabled to make contact with the root and core issues which constitute psychological stagnation and irresponsibility in the context of adult-youth relationships in South Africa. The black church in South Africa needs to come to terms with the fact in more serious terms than ever before that the problem in question has moral and ethical connotations. This calls for a restructuring of the current methods of doing pastoral care. My contribution to this is to aid black South African pastors to use the insights of Erikson's life cycle theory and Niebuhr's ethics of responsibility to render a more relevant form of pastoral care to black adults and youth. At the same time we should heed the warning of Paul Pruyser in his book *The Minister as Diagnostician*.[8] He warns that the pastor who wants to play psychologist will do his helpee a great disservice. "I believe that problem-laden persons who seek help from a pastor do so for very deep reasons--from the desire to look at themselves in a theological perspective."[9] The minister has the responsibility to meet this need according to Dr. Pruyser. However, while the pastor attempts a theological diagnosis with the aid of faith symbols the insights of psychology, e.g., Erikson's personality theory could be brought into play as problems are never strictly theological or psychological by nature. Oftentimes psychological discipline enhances theological diagnosis and vice versa.

In the book *Practical Theology*.[10] edited by Don Browning, the significance of theological ethics for pastoral theology and pastoral care is emphasized in every chapter. In his essay entitled "Pastoral Theology in a Pluralistic Age,"[11] Browning writes: "Pastoral Theology should rediscover itself as a dimension of theological or religious ethics. It is the primary task of pastoral theology to bring together theological ethics and the social sciences to articulate a normative vision of the human life cycle."[12] In his essay, "Practical Theology and Pastoral Care: An Essay in Pastoral Theology"[13] we discern a healthy tension between Browning and Lapsley concerning the relationship of pastoral theology to ethics. Lapsley declares that, "The central characteristic of any theory of pastoral care must be the discernment of and appropriate strategies and tactics for attaining the possibilities for a particular person or persons. . . It is this emphasis upon the possibilities, and hence, also, limits, for particular persons that gives pastoral theology its peculiar identity among theological disciplines. It is also this emphasis that provides its distinction from ethics. Pastoral theology is not a branch of ethics. . . ."[14] However both authors see the important role played by ethics in undergirding pastoral theology. In their article, "Interdependence of the Pastoral and the Prophetic," Clinebell and Seifert emphasize a corrective perspective for the traditional methods of caring.

> It is clear that both the focus on helping individuals and the focus on working to change person-damaging social conditions are indispensable aspects of the mission of the church.[15]

While they do not declare so directly these two authors convey the fact that this mission or caring function of the church cannot be executed without taking into consideration the role that theological ethics plays in this regard. It thus becomes clear that there is an urgent need to restructure the method of doing pastoral care in the black church in South Africa. This book is therefore an inquiry into Erikson's psychosocial theory and Niebuhr's ethics of responsibility to ascertain how these two disciplines could aid the execution of a more relevant approach to pastoral care to black adults in South Africa. This book furthermore wants to ascertain in which way it could enable black adults to be more generative and more responsible to their youth in a society that limits their range for ethical action, and which causes life to be devoid of meaning for such individuals. Gerkin says that the pastor needs to be an interpreter and a guide [to these black adults] who are so deeply troubled (brackets are mine).[16] The following words of Gerkin portray something of what black adults in South Africa are experiencing, what they yearn for:

> In the midst of this givenness of our individual situation, each of us must, if we are to live with any integrity at all, somehow on the other hand retain a sense of our own agency, our own ability to do and be someone with power to act and *choose*. It is at this point that the human capacity to make meaning comes into play. We must exercise our need and capacity to make *meaningful interpretations* of who we are, what the world is, and what, given our situation, is most meaningful--what Tillich calls our ultimate concern.[17]

Black adults in South Africa need to have their sense of agency which is interwoven with a sense of responsibility and responsiveness affirmed. They also have a need to be guided to make interpretations of their day-to-day existence that make sense to them in the morally stagnant socio-political situation that they encounter from day to day. It is my conviction that if we isolate the 7th stage in Erikson's life cycle theory, namely the adult stage of Generativity vs. Stagnation, and focus upon it from a psycho-dynamic perspective while we simultaneously focus on Niebuhr's metaphor of the Responsible Self, we would be moving closer to the much needed goal of enabling these individuals to receive a sense of their own agency, to make meaningful interpretations of their life situations and to be able to act generatively and responsibly to their youth even when their range for ethical action is deliberately and severely curtailed. In this book we will we will try to show how this could possibly be achieved with the aid of an instrument of analysis which will be called an ethical-psychological model of interpretation in chapter 3.

Choice of Psychologist

I choose Erikson for the following reasons:

1)   The formation of identity is central to his psychosocial theory. This aspect of his theory is of crucial importance to this study as it focuses on the struggle of black South African adults to give their youth a clear and positive identity.

2) Most black South African adults are struggling to achieve a sense of generativity. Erikson deals with this psychological dynamic in great detail.

3) The problem of ungenerativity or stagnation as Erikson calls it pertains to the development of human personality. Erikson is very helpful in this regard as he is one of the best known personality theorists. He has studied the evolution of personalities of different cultures, e.g., the Sioux and Yurok Indians on the Pacific Coast and South

Dakota respectively, Martin Luther, a German, Mahatma
Gandhi, and Indian, and he gave the T. B. Davies lecture at
the University of Cape Town in South Africa.   His
knowledge of other cultures as well as his studies of
personalities that evolved in situations of social change and
social conflict make him a good choice for this study.

4) Generativity and Stagnation are developmental
issues. As Erikson focuses on developmental factors in the
human life cycle (children and adults) his theory is
appropriate.

5)   Another focus of this book is on parent-child
relationships in conflict situations and the difficulties that
are experienced with the achieving of a clear identity in
such contexts. Erikson has done such studies. The reader
is specifically referred to his book, *Young Man Luther*[18]

6) Finally, Erikson has done thorough studies on
Adulthood and Youth.   In this regard the readers are
referred to his book, *Identity, Youth and Crisis*.

Choice of Ethicist

1) I chose H. Richard Niebuhr as an ethicist to work
with as he is interested in the moral life. Special emphasis
is placed on his book entitled *The Responsible Self, An
Essay in Christian Moral Philosophy*. Philosophy as it is
used in this regard means understanding. This book is thus
". . . the reflections of a Christian who is seeking to
understand the mode of his existence and that of his fellow
beings as human agents."[19] In this book we are looking at
black Christians in South Africa who are seeking to
understand their moral lives. The relevance of Niebuhr's
work is therefore obvious.   "It is a phenomenological
analysis of man's moral existence."[20]

2) Several prominent themes prevail in this book which are all imperative for the understanding of the moral lives of the group of people in South Africa who are the main characters in this book, namely:

2.1:   "The Center of Value" or God and the individual or a community's relationship to him.
2.2:   Ethical analysis as an aid to those who struggle to achieve integrity in their lives.
2.3:   The place of the Bible in theological ethics.
2.4:   Radical Monotheism.
2.5:   Response to our fellow man and response to God.
2.6:   The Dynamic Triad of Faith.
2.7:   The analysis of the self as responsive and responsible in its social character.
2.8:   Selfhood as understood by Niebuhr.
2.9:   Loyalty and Commitment to a Cause.
2.10: The Self as a Social Being.

3) Niebuhr also enables me to understand how people respond in a closed society. South Africa is a closed society. Thus Niebuhr shares some valuable moral, ethical, and Biblical insights.

4) In the section entitled "Jesus as the paradigm of responsibility" Niebuhr gives us the greatest norm for moral reflection and understanding in South Africa.
5) By means of his metaphor of the Responsible Self, Niebuhr places the entire moral struggle of black adults in South Africa in balanced perspective and rings out chords of faith, hope, self-understanding, forgiveness, and reconciliation which are all much needed elements in order for God's Kingdom to come in a troubled land, as well as integrity, responsibility, and generativity.

Outlines of Chapters

Chapter 1: A detailed description of Erikson's psychosocial theory is given with special emphasis on the 7th stage, that is, the adult stage of generativity vs. stagnation.

Chapter 2: A detailed description of Niebuhr's ethics of responsibility is given. Certain themes are highlighted to show how they are intricately interwoven with the moral struggle of black adults in South Africa, e.g., "The Center of Value," Radical Monotheism, Selfhood, and the Dynamic Triad of Faith.

Chapter 3: An ethical-psychological model is constructed for use as an instrument of analysis of the moral and psychological lives of certain black adults in South Africa. The human pole (psychology) is compared to the divine pole (ethics). A correlation is made between faith and identity in a dynamic way. The relationship between responsibility and generativity is discussed in depth.

Chapter 4: Here we have the stories of five black adults which could be regarded as a microcosm of the lives of the average black adult in South Africa.

These stories were recorded with a microcassette recorder under difficult circumstances. The author visited South Africa in December 1985/January 1986 and personally conducted the interviews. He was introduced to many people by friends who were colleagues in the ministry in South Africa. Most of the people interviewed were parishioners of various pastor friends of the author. In spite of that fact, much suspicion prevailed, particularly at the sight of a tape recorder. In the end the five stories chosen for the fourth chapter stood out as those that best represented the struggle, moral and psychological, that most black adults were going through at that time. A State of

Emergency was in effect at that time and the atmosphere in the country was one of tension, fear, and mistrust.

Five verbatims are presented. The following questions based on the book of John Kotre, *Outliving the Self*,[21] were presented to the interviewees:

1.   If you looked at your life as a story that came in chapters what would those chapters be?

2.   How does a parent care for a child in a crisis situation, particularly the current one of violence and unrest?

3.   Does the South African situation limit your parenting function?

4.   Has your personality changed over the past ten years?

The questions were asked in the context of Niebuhr's ethics of responsibility and Erikson's generativity vs. stagnation stage to ascertain how generative/stagnant or responsible/irresponsible the relationship of black adults was towards their children.

All five stories were analyzed by means of my ethical-psychological model. A general ethical-psychological summary of the five cases is presented at the end of chapter four.

Chapter 5: this is our constructive chapter. an application of the insights gained from our research into responsibility and generativity is made to the situation, particularly the relationships between black adults and their children. The question: Can black adults be fully generative and fully responsible and responsive to their youth, given the fact that their range for ethical action is severely curtailed in South Africa, is answered. Various moral and psychological dynamics are highlighted.

METHOD

This book is concerned with the fact that pastors in South Africa are giving pastoral care to black adults by means of the application of impoverished methods that have been in practice for generations. Browning says, "Care is a complex practical activity. Like any practical action, it is composed of several levels of reasoning and decision."[22] Quoting from Peter Berger's book, *The Sacred Canopy*[23] he says that in the face of modernity, institutional differentiation, and pluralism, "the plausible structures" of society collapse. When this occurs, "we can no longer unreflectively rely on the received tradition to guide our practical activity."[24] ". . . Under the pressure of conflict and crisis we begin thinking about the tradition critically."[25]

I am concerned that a concerted effort should be made to overcome this deficiency. My method wants to develop an argument for reconstituting our traditions of care by introducing psychological, moral, and ethical concerns directly into pastoral care and counseling in South Africa. There should be inherent in our pastoral care and counseling methods a vigorous ethical and moral confrontation of situations that require pastoral care, in particular the ungenerative and irresponsible/unresponsive parent-child situation in South Africa. Such an approach could have a more positive outcome for handling the problem(s) in question.

The primary purpose of this book is to identify if ungenerativity also referred to as self-absorption and stagnation by Erikson as well as irresponsibility/ unresponsiveness occur between black South African adults and their children, particularly their youth. This identification will be done against the background of a situation of rapid social change and crisis in South

Africa--one in which the range for ethical action of such adults is greatly curtailed by the society that dominates their existence.

The method in this book is an ETHICAL-PSYCHO-LOGICAL INVESTIGATION in which the life stories of a number of black South African adults were recorded and analyzed from an ethical-psychological perspective. The manner in which generativity/self-absorption and irresponsibility is used is to indicate a lack of adequate care in the sense of preparing the ensuing generation to face their world adequately by being prepared developmentally, morally, and ethically. While we recognize that this is not the only way to care for black South African youth, we believe that these are two of the most crucial spheres of life which need the attention of pastoral care.

This book is focused on parent-child relationships in a particular context. Responsibility and generativity are the basic criteria which are used to assess the positive and negative psychological and moral/ethical dynamics that occur in that relationship. We want to ascertain what is taking place during the processes of generativity and responsibility in the context of this relationship.

This method is partially *dialectic* in nature. In this regard we use the term dialectic to indicate a degree of tension and similarities that exists between the ethical-psychological or the divine and human poles of our model or instrument of analysis respectively (chapter 3 of book). It will become evident that there is a degree of dialecticism between faith and identity.

Analogical analysis also forms part of our method. The author of this book will place the divine (vertical, ethical) pole in a relationship with the (horizontal, human, psychological) pole. Such a relationship will indicate clearly that faith and identity are related to each other at points that are common to them. By means of analogy I will reveal in a systematic way that points of congruence and dissimilarities exist between the horizontal and vertical dimensions of this book.

The dialectic aspect of our method enables the divine and human poles to gain insights from each other's perspectives. Responsibility functions horizontally and vertically as follows: Horizontally (self-other selves/social companions); self-God/God-self as well as social companions or other selves and vice versa. Generativity operates horizontally as follows: Parents-children; and vertically: parents-God also referred to as "this sense of a hallowed presence...a pervasive element which is best called the numinous."[26] The reverse also occurs from God to parents.

My contribution in this book occurs due to the fact that I allow Browning's religio-theological-moral perspective of pastoral care and Erikson's psychosocial theory as well as Niebuhr's ethics of responsibility to indicate that the traditional methods of pastoral care to black adults in South Africa are deficient. This is due to the fact that it has neglected to employ the insights of psychology and ethics. By reconstructing our pastoral care methods in South Africa as I have attempted to do in this book, with the aid of Erikson and Niebuhr, a more relevant form of pastoral care could evolve which could restore integrity, wholeness, meaning, generativity, and responsibility in the lives of black adults.

This in turn could lead to healthier parent-child relationships in South Africa. Insights gained from this book, in particular from the ethical-psychological model that I constructed, could aid pastoral care in other situations of rapid social change and social conflict in the world. Ultimately, I am making a contribution to what Browning refers to as *The Moral Context of Pastoral Care.*

A limitation of this book is the fact that I did not place adequate emphasis on the actions of black South African women in the situation of moral conflict and choice under discussion. This was not intentional. Erikson expands on Freud's theory of psychoanalysis which is male oriented. Thus, he places greater emphasis on the male than on the female child.

It is worth noting what Carol Gilligan says about this. She writes:

> "Yet despite Erikson's observation of sex differences, his chart of life-cycle stages remains unchanged: identity continues to precede intimacy as male experience continues to define his life-cycle conception. But in the male cycle there is little preparation for the intimacy of the first adult stage...attachments appear to be developmental impediments, as is repeatedly the case in the assessment of women."[27]

Gilligan cautions that we should be careful not to regard male behavior as the norm and female behavior as a deviation from that norm. She refers to the "missing text of women's development" which she is attempting to restore. She says "In focussing primarily on the differences between the accounts of women and men, my aim is to enlarge developmental understanding by including the perspectives of both of the sexes."[28]

I am in full agreement with Dr. Gilligan regarding the latter quotation. However, I trust that in spite of the shortcomings of this book that I have at least provided some impetus for further discussion on a very crucial subject.

CHAPTER 1

Erikson's Life Cycle Theory

Erikson's life cycle theory is built on Freud's analytic theory. He refers to Freud's work as the "rock" on which all advancement of personality theory is based.[1]

Erikson's theory is not just an extension of Freud's. He goes further than Freud by including the stages of adulthood. His theory diverges from Freud's due to the prominence that he gives to the following three areas. First, there is the emphasis he places on the ego rather than the id.[2] It is interesting to note that Erikson speaks about his first book, *Childhood and Society,* as a "psychoanalytic book on the relations of the ego to society."[3]

Secondly, Erikson introduces a new matrix, the individual in his relationship to his parents within the context of the family and in relation to a wider social setting within the framework of the family's historical-cultural heritage.[4] In this regard he moves away from Freud's emphasis on the individual.

Thirdly, whereas Freud strongly emphasizes the role and function of the unconscious, Erikson focusses on interpersonal relations.

It is important to look at the assumptions that are basic to Erikson's theory. Henry Maier explains it nicely in his book *Three Theories of Child Development.*[5] Here is a brief treatise.

1. *Approach to theory formation*
    In order to gather his data Erikson employs psychoanalytic methods and techniques. He applies the methods of psychoanalysis to groups of people as well as to entire cultures. For him, play is the best context in which to analyze the ego of the child. His theory is based on data that he gains from his own observations of specific problems. He also makes use of cultural anthropology, history, and Freudian psychology.

2. *Order of human life*

"Erikson concedes that in naming a series of basic balances on which psychosocial health of a personality seems to depend, I found myself implying a latent universal value system which is based on the nature of human growth, the needs of the developing ego, and certain common elements in childrearing systems."[6]

Erikson assumes that in the organism there is a unification of biological, psychological, and social forces. He believes that in the psychogenetic life cycle of every person there is a repetitive pattern of his phylogenetic evolution, e.g., ingestion or incorporation is the primary function of the primitive organisms. The infant just like the jellyfish has the same primary function, that is, incorporation. There are parallel dynamics between the development of as well as the human's phylogenetic evolution. "Personality development follows biological" as well as cultural principles.

3. *Fundamental human values*

Erikson believes in "the creative and adaptive power of the individual."[7]

The sanctity of the individual is dependent on the trust and respect of the culture and the society that surrounds it. Similarly, for social institutions to survive they must receive "respect and recognition from individuals who depend upon them."[8] There is thus a reciprocal relationship between the individual and the world in which it interacts socially.

4. *Etiology of human behavior*

Erikson and Freud are in agreement about the fact that the human being possesses psychosexual energy. This energy is a strong motivating force or drive in the person which both of them refer to as libido. Maier explains libidinal energy as an unknown force which guides the epigenetic development of the person. Both Erikson and Freud recognize that there are unconscious life experiences to which libidinal forces become attached. But Erikson believes that these drives can be adapted to different unlimited life patterns.

5. *The core of human functioning*
     Erikson believes that the quality or the nature of the libidinal, which could also be called the emotional, forms the core of the functions of the human body, that is, the id, the ego, and the superego determine how a person will live his/her life. Erikson attaches great importance to child's play. He regards it as being very important for the development of the child. "Play is the ego's acceptable tool for self-expression."[9]

6. *The newborn*
     According to Erikson the newborn baby possesses personality from a psychological point of view. The environment has a great effect on the child at birth. The child and its family both have a reciprocal effect on each other.

7. *Physical, social, cultural, and ideational environments*
     The individual's personality is also shaped by physical, social, cultural, and ideational factors in his or her environment, according to Erikson. In such an environment helping adults, e.g., parents, are important for the maintenance of a balance of the child's behavior and learning, etc. In the ideational sphere religion and ideology help the child to find meaning beyond the limits of reason.

The Stages
     Erikson describes human development in terms of eight psychosocial stages. He uses the word cycle to "convey the double tendency of individual life to round itself out as a coherent experience and at the same time to form a link in the chain of generations from which it receives and to which it contributes both strengths and weaknesses."[10] This

point suggests that it is not Erikson's intention to focus on the life cycle of the individual as such, but he wishes to place the emphasis on the "cycle of generations" or on the interplay of the life cycles of different generations. He says that there is a "cog-wheeling" or interlocking process that takes place between preceding and succeeding generations.

According to Erikson the growth of human beings takes place in a sequence of eight stages which evolve into a psychosocial personality. He views the life cycle as an integrated psychosocial phenomenon rather than following "what in analogy to teleology may be called the origino-logical" approach to derive the meaning of development primarily from a reconstruction of the infant's beginning.[11]

A very important element in this theory is the EPIGENETIC PRINCIPLE.

> ...this principle states that anything that grows has a ground plan, and that out of this ground plan the parts arise, each part having its time of special ascendancy, until all parts have arisen to form a functioning whole.[12]

In light of this principle every stage of growth is connected to the other stages of the life cycle. The stages all follow a proper pattern and every stage is already present in a particular manner and remains in that particular manner or state until the person encounters the social world from the perspective of that stage. This encounter results in a critical phase in the developmental history of the individual and it in turn brings about a perspectival change in the individual.

The person now sees the world differently and responds to it in a different manner. Erikson refers to these different stages of growth as psychosocial modalities, e.g., learning how to *get* and how to *give* in the first stage and learning how to be generative or to *care* for others in the

7th stage. Erikson also believes that the Epigenetic Principle is responsible for the predetermined sequence of the stages. Furthermore, the presence of this principle in the stage theory means that a positive or negative environment can be constructive or destructive to human development.

Every stage is bi-polar. At every stage there is a negative and a positive pole. The positive poles are referred to as strengths by Erikson and the negative ones as weaknesses. For healthy human development to take place the positive pole must be stronger than the negative one. The ego plays a very dynamic role in this theory. It has the power to integrate or to synthesize. This power enables it to provide strong links for and between the stages. In each stage of development there are two opposing forces that coexist and they require a joint solution or synthesis. The real challenge of the ego is found in the coexistence of these two forces. The successful synthesis of two opposing senses in a developmental phase enables the individual to achieve or acquire or "achieving a positive sense of, that is, a notion of competency in the spheres most relevant at that particular point of development...."[13]

A point of concern is Erikson's use of the word "versus," e.g., trust vs. mistrust in the first stage. It could be misleading or unsettling. The impression could be conveyed that the pulls in opposite directions are seeking to neutralize each other. But this is not so. The negative pole is a "disharmony," but necessary. Of utmost importance is the ratio between the positive and the negative poles.

One may easily get the impression that human development is characterized by a sequence of crises. But Erikson states clearly that this is not so.

> We do not consider all development a series of crises: we claim only that psychosocial development proceeds by critical steps, "critical" being a characteristic of turning points, of

moments of decision between progress and
regression, integration and retardation.[14]

The beautiful aspect of Erikson's theory is the fact
that inherent in it is the propensity for overcoming these
crises by means of the new strengths or virtues that are
accrued simultaneously at every crisis point leading to
greater growth and integration in the personality. Erikson
says further that a new vice crops up at every stage of life
and these act as obstacles in the individual's way of
achieving moral order in his/her life. Erikson is reluctant
to employ terms like "vice" or "sin" for these negative traits
in the person's personality. He prefers to use the term
antipathies to describe the vices that are in opposition to
the virtues that evolve at each step of the development of
the person's personality.   In his book *The Life Cycle
Completed*,[15] he gives a clear chart which describes among
others, these antipathies.   They are: withdrawal,
compulsion, inhibition, inertia, repudiation, exclusivity,
rejectivity, and wisdom. The stages in the life cycle that
correspond to these antipathies in the same order are:
infancy, early childhood, play age, school age, adolescence,
young adulthood, adulthood, the old age. The psychosocial
crises that correspond to them in the exact order as they are
listed are: basic trust vs. basic mistrust, autonomy vs.
shame and doubt, initiative vs. guilt, industry vs. inferiority,
identity vs. identity confusion, intimacy vs. isolation,
generativity vs. stagnation, integrity vs. despair.

Stage 1: *Basic Trust vs. Basic Mistrust*
        This stage occurs in the infant stage. The first task
of the ego is to resolve the nuclear conflict of basic trust vs.
basic mistrust. The degree of trust that the infant develops
during this stage depends on the quality of the relationship
with its mother.

> Mothers create a sense of trust in their children
> by that kind of administration which in its
> quality combines sensitive care of the baby's
> individual needs . . . culture's life style.[16]

This relationship also forms the basis of the child's sense of identity. The outcome of this stage depends on how the emotional and physical needs of the child are met. Physically the child needs to be fed because it is very dependent on the mother and it needs to be loved emotionally too. The quality of the care of the parents gives the child a feeling of well-being and security. Through it the child learns to trust the world and the people in its environment.

When the relationship between the infant and its parents is characterized by lack of affection, basic mistrust in the world will result. When basic trust is the outcome of the first stage, it expresses the fact that there is integration between child and parent. In order for a child to develop into a stable and confident person there needs to be a good emotional climate in which this can grow. It thus becomes clear that the first task of development of the human personality is to acquire basic trust in the people with whom it interacts in the world.

The mother-child context is very important for the psychosocial development of the child, e.g., in this context the child learns the social modality "to get." The first thing that the infant is able to achieve socially is to allow its mother to leave its visual ambit without protest "because she has become an inner certainty as well as an outer predictability."[17]

The development of basic trust is a major psychosocial task in infancy and the mother-child context is the matrix where this takes place and is developed. The mature faith of the adult in later life begins with the resolution of the basic trust vs. basic mistrust conflict in the first stage. The virtue that develops during this stage is *hope*. Erikson believes this to be the most indispensable of all the virtues of his life cycle theory as it is the one by means of which life is sustained. For hope to develop the infant must have a relationship with parents who are trustworthy. These parents should also respond to its needs with warmth and love.

Stage 2: *Autonomy vs. Shame and Doubt*
    Erikson's second stage is based on the assumption that there is a conflict between autonomy vs. shame and doubt and that this gives rise to the virtue of will and self-control.

> Will, therefore, is the unbroken determination to exercise free choice as well as self-restraint, in spite of the unavoidable experience of shame and doubt in infancy.[18]

Freud's theory characterizes this stage as anal. This stage also helps the child to form a sense of psychosocial independence when it is viewed from the angle of the ego. Erikson mentions the fact that two contradictory modes prevail during this stage, viz. *retention* and *elimination*. This whole stage with its accompanying anal problem becomes a struggle for autonomy. The child struggles to stand on its feet by itself. Its world takes on another characteristic now, namely, "I," "You," and "Me."[19]
    Erikson says that if the conflict between autonomy vs. shame and doubt is not resolved there may be more shame than autonomy. The result will be that such a person will suffer from an inferiority complex all his/her life or spend the rest of his/her life fighting such feelings. An important biological development of this stage is the maturation of the muscle system which makes possible the voluntary evacuation of the bowels and bladder. This "holding on" and "letting go" helps to give rise to the

autonomous will of the child, according to Erikson. This whole stage, then, becomes a battle for autonomy.[20]

If the parent by gentle and loving encouragement allows the child to gain a sense of self-control over the sphincters without the loss of self-esteem the child will develop a permanent sense of autonomy and pride. If the parents exercise too much control, there will be a permanent sense of doubt and shame: "Shame supposes that one is completely exposed and conscious of being looked at...in a word self-conscious."[21]

Stage 3: *Initiative vs. Guilt*

At about age 3 or 4 years the child is ready to proceed to the next stage after solving the autonomy vs. shame/doubt conflict. There seems to be a more harmonious growth in the psychological and physical makeup of the child. The child suddenly wants to learn and do more things. It also has a strong sense of initiative at this stage. At the same time, there arises a sense of guilt due to new goals that have been set for the self. The child also moves about more vigorously and acquires greater mastery over language. This in turn broadens the horizons of his imagination. All of this helps to face the next crisis in a better way. A large part of the child's behavior at this stage is intrusive in nature.

> These include the intrusion into other bodies by physical attack; the intrusion into other people's ears and minds by aggressive talking; the intrusion into space by vigorous locomotion; the intrusion into the unknown by consuming curiosity.[22]

As part of his struggle for autonomy the child concentrates on the exclusion of rivals from its territory, e.g., younger siblings as they are viewed as obstacles in the way of the object on which his initiative is focused, namely

the mother. If this initiative does not succeed, guilt occurs.
At the same time the child develops its morality and a
conscience, that governor of initiative, which is responsible
for the child's experiencing a sense of guilt during this
stage.   By using the initiative vs. guilt stage, Erikson
intended to supplement Freud's stage of the Oedipus crisis.

> Therefore, for Erikson oedipal problems are the
> infantile or neurotic manifestation of generational
> conflict, which is unavoidable in human beings
> who experience life in terms of successive
> generations.[23]

Stage 4: *Industry vs. Inferiority*
       During this stage the child produces things by which
he/she learns to win recognition. He develops more skills
which are applied to given tasks.

> He develops a sense of industry, that is, he
> adjusts himself to the inorganic laws of the tool
> world.[24]

The child's ego boundaries have expanded and they now
include tools and skills. He also takes the work principle
more to heart. By means of it, he learns that completed
work brings certain pleasures when one consistently
perseveres at it. However, the child faces a problem at this
stage, namely, a feeling of inadequacy, a feeling of
inferiority. This is brought about when he feels that he is
incapable of mastering his tools and his skills.   He
experiences a sense of isolation and withdrawal. It is at
this point where he needs the parent and society.
       Another crucial factor at this stage is that here in
his psychosocial stage the child learns to cooperate with
others in the making of things. Erikson refers to it as an
awareness of a division of labor and a sense of the
chronological ethos of culture.[25] According to Erikson, guilt
and low self-worth/esteem can also set in here when the

child is made to feel, for example, that his pigmentation and the social status of his parents are the deciding factors or norms for his efficiency as an apprentice and for his sense of identity.

This causes the child to impose self-restrictions which will have a negative psychological effect on his performance, social interaction, and self-esteem in later life and particularly in adulthood. In this latter stage such a child would have developed an ungenerative or stagnant personality. He would also have difficulty with the task of responsibility due to a limited range for ethical action. And because there is a cogwheeling of the stages of adult and youth this will create intergenerational conflict.

Erikson says that this stage can be characterized by "I am what I learn."[26]

Stage 5: *Identity vs. Role Confusion*

The onset of puberty and the building up of a solid relationship with the universe of tools marks the end of childhood and the advent of youth. The child now experiences rapid growth in its body, physiological maturation as well as the maturing of the genitals. The child now has an obsession with the manner in which he is viewed by other people as compared to the way they feel about themselves. They are also concerned about how to make the roles and skills they acquired earlier on more meaningful.

There is now a struggle within the psyche of the youth for integration in the form of ego-identity.

> The sense of ego identity, then, is the accrued confidence that the inner sameness and continuity prepared in the past are matched by the sameness and continuity of one's meaning for others....[27]

The acute crisis that comes about in this stage is role
confusion.   Young people experience great difficulty in
deciding on an appropriate occupational identity.   This
problem throws them off balance psychologically.   In order
to restore their equilibrium they indulge in over-
identification with "the heroes of cliques and crowds."
Erikson believes that falling in love at this stage should be
seen as part of the struggle of youth to establish an identity.
They do this by projecting their diffused ego image onto the
object of their struggle, that is, the girl or boyfriend.   They
receive a partial solution to their problem by seeing it
"reflected and gradually clarified."

Erikson says further that when young people become
clannish by rejecting people who are different from them,
e.g., in pigmentation or religious affiliation, etc., it should be
seen as a defense mechanism against their problem of
identity confusion.   This stage is also the testing ground or
a period of experimentation and a time for making
mistakes.   Erikson refers to this stage as a moratorium.   It
is:

> ...a psychosocial stage between childhood and
> adulthood, and between the morality learned by
> the child, and the ethics to be developed by the
> adult....It is an ideological mind.   In searching for
> the social values which guide identity, one
> therefore confronts problems of ideology and
> aristocracy.[28]

It becomes clear that the different stages of
Erikson's theory are interwoven or "cogwheeled."   Ego
identity is firmly linked to the first stage of trust vs.
mistrust where the virtue of hope is born.   On the other
hand, the adult stage is also an important aid for the
understanding of the identity vs. identity diffusion stage as
it is the generative adult who gives the youth their identity.
Erikson says,

> A lasting ego identity cannot begin to exist
> without the trust of the first oral stage; it cannot
> be completed without a promise of fulfillment
> which from the dominant image of adulthood
> reaches down into the baby's beginnings and
> which creates at every step an accruing sense of
> ego strength.[29]

Another crisis that occurs in this stage is identity
diffusion. If a young person cannot find "sameness and
continuity" identity diffusion occurs. Charles Kao says that
identity diffusion is the inability to integrate all dimensions
of experiences in the past into a meaningful hierarchical
whole.[30]

During this adolescent stage, ideology also plays a
very important role. The young person searches around for
people and ideas that they can have faith in. The onset of
adolescence causes a break to occur in the continuity of the
life cycle processes and the different stages. The adolescent
now wants to restore that continuity, but in a new way.
This restoration process is full of tension and anxiety
because the adolescent also wants a way that will include
his new sexual maturity. There is also a need to integrate
all the "basic building blocks" that are needed for identity
formation that were acquired in the preceding stages, e.g.,
trust, hope, will, etc. At the same time the adolescent
experiences conflict due to the fact that he does not want to
make a blind, overzealous commitment which might create
doubt in his psyche.

One detects a sense of intolerance on the part of
adolescents. This should not be regarded as willful as it is
oftentimes a defense mechanism to resist identity loss.[31]
This identity loss is aggravated even more by rapid body
changes, e.g., overwhelming genital maturation, and its
accompanying responsibilities and a future that suddenly
looms up ahead with numerous conflicting opportunities and
alternatives. Dealing with these scary problems from

within the parameters of a group or clique is "safer" and the group acts as a support system under stressful conditions.

Erikson moves beyond Freud in his understanding of and in his analysis of identity and the identity crisis. While Freud stresses the adjustment of the personality, Erikson stresses adaptation. In this way he moves from Freud's pathological point of departure in studying identity crisis to normative health. Erikson's whole eight-stage theory describes the healthy and not the pathological personality like Freud does. This is also an important point that shows how and where Erikson's and Freud's methodologies differ from each other.

Freud

There is, however, not a complete break between Erikson and Freud. Erikson finds Freud helpful to explain part of his view of identity.

Freud first used the term identity in a serious way and in a central ethical sense in 1926 when he addressed the Society of B'nai B'rith in Vienna. What he said in that address has helped Erikson in his understanding of identity and to formulate his own definition.

Freud referred to "many obscure emotional forces which were the more powerful the less they could be expressed in words, as well as a clear consciousness of inner identity, the safe privacy of a common mental construction."[32] For Freud, to be in possession of an inner identity also included a great sense of pride that the Jews clung to in spite of all the persecution they endured. Furthermore, Freud contrasted "the positive identity of a fearless freedom of thinking with a negative trait in the peoples among whom we Jews live."[33]

Erikson says that this suggests that the identity of a person or a group may be relative to that of another. It is an indication of an inner liberation from a more dominant group I.D. when a person has a pride of gaining a strong identity.[34]

William James

William James also initially used a psychology on which our current thinking on identity is based. But James used the word character to describe a sense of identity, something that can be experienced and something that "comes upon you." Erikson says, "One can study in James' life history a protracted identity crisis as well as the emergence of a 'self-made' identity in a new and expansive American civilization."[35]   Both Freud and James have helped to establish a number of dimensions of identity. At the same time they give us insight into the reason why identity is so difficult to grasp. The basic reason for the difficulty is due to the fact that the process of identity is grounded in the individual and in his culture. This process "establishes the identity of these two identities."[36]

In his book *Young Man Luther*[37] Erikson uses his method in concrete terms. He illustrates how Luther solved an acute identity crisis by the adaptation of his ego. When looking at identity, Erikson's psychoanalytic vision moves across the border of youth. He says that the older generation has the responsibility of giving youth an ideology that they can identify with. Erikson says that identity is a generational issue, not one generation, but different generations.[38]

The *Identity Crisis* occurs where there is a sense of discontinuity and when this is experienced between the person and society. On the physiological side the person has changed and he suddenly realizes that he is no longer in childhood. He is now confronted with relations that involve sexual intimacy and career responsibility. He can only face these when he has a sense of trust which he acquired in his childhood stages. "Career" choice, which is a demand of society on the youth, is regarded by Erikson as one of the basic factors in the identity crisis. The uncertainty and anxiety in the youth/young person make it a very scary experience to face up to this societal demand. To explain the period during which the young person tries to work through his uncertainties and anxieties Erikson employs the term *moratorium*.

> The adolescent mind is essentially a mind of the moratorium, a psychosocial stage between childhood and adulthood and between the morality learned by the child, and the ethics to be developed by the adult. It is an ideological mind....[39]

During the moratorium period the youth can experiment with behavioral traits which are a mixture of youthful and adult behavior while at the same time discovering some links between his usual behavior and those which evolve as a result of his involvement with new ideologies. This moratorium period is vital to the young person's psychosocial development. It gives him/her the opportunity to incorporate identity factors that he learned during the prior stages into his adolescent identity which is evolving at this time. This will contribute positively to the way in which he will relate to society at that point and in the ensuing periods. A partial function of the moratorium is to enable the young person to find values that are meaningful to him/her.

The young person who is caught up in an identity crisis will remain restless until he finds an ideology to which he may pledge his fidelity. Fidelity is the strength that arises during this particular stage. With the aid of ideology the young person tries to find meaning in life. Ideology always evokes a response in youth which could be positive or negative. Through ideology the young person hopes to find a view of the world that makes sense to him and to which he can commit himself fully. Erikson defines ideology as follows:

> A living ideology is a systematized set of ideas and ideals which unifies the striving for psychosocial identity...official ideology.[40]

A fact that is often overlooked is that identity formation is rooted in the social matrix. Erikson stressed this and in this way he moved beyond Freud's explanations.

Stages 6, 7, and 8: Adulthood Stages
     In Erikson's theory adulthood has three stages. It is in the adulthood section of his theory where it becomes clear how far Erikson has moved beyond Freud and his psychosocial focus in childhood. Adulthood consists of more than one stage, namely: the intimacy vs. isolation stage; generativity vs. stagnation stage; and the ego integrity vs. despair stage. Each stage has its own specific crisis. Much research still needs to be done on adulthood. It was Erikson's driving force, clinical creativity, and inspiration that gave rise to the fact that an entire issue of *Daedalus* covered the Adulthood Stage.[41] He also wrote with depth and insight about two famous adults, namely Gandhi and Dr. Borg, in which he analyzed adulthood psycho-analytically.[42]

Stage 6: *Intimacy vs. Isolation*
     The young person is now ready to allow his identity to be fused with that of other people. In other words, he is willing to have an intimate relationship with others. Erikson refers to intimacy as:

> ...the capacity to commit himself to concrete affiliations and partnerships and to develop the ethical strength to abide by such commitments, even though they may call for significant sacrifices and compromises...self-absorption.[43]

Distantiation is the opposing or negative sense of intimacy. Erikson explains distantiation as the moves by the individual to push some people away from him and even to act in a destructive way toward them. But this same isolator can also be intimate and hostile to the same person.

Erikson says that true genitality also develops at this stage. The genital forces that operated in the person before this period are used by the young person in his quest to find an identity. By genitality Erikson means:

> The unobstructed capacity to develop an orgastic potency to free...tensions from body.[44]

Isolation is the danger which comes at this stage by which the person steers clear of relationships which focus on intimacy.

Stage 7: *Generativity vs. Stagnation*

> Generativity, then, is primarily the concern in establishing and guiding the next generation... cannot replace it.[45]

The opposing sense of generativity is stagnation. It is a form of regression. It adversely affects interpersonal relationships. When people are unable to be generative they become self-indulgent and act as if they were their own and only child. Erikson says that there are parents who are unable to be generative for various reasons which can be traced back to indelible impressions that stem from the phase of early childhood, e.g., negative identification with parents; excessive self-love which stems from a too rigid self-made personality; and an absence of faith in the species.[46]

Generativity and stagnation should not be limited to the narrow confines of the process of procreation but it should be seen in the light of Erikson's explanation, namely, it refers to the direction that is set and followed by parents, in the context of their society, so that the generation that follows may profit from the virtues that they have acquired over the years.[47]

Generativity, furthermore, also means that adults and parents will assume responsibility for the contribution that their society makes to care for the next generation, e.g., education, health care, care of the environment, etc. However, it is only when a mutuality and a relationship of trust exist between the adult and his/her community that real care can evolve or becomes possible. That means that their personal, creative, and ideational life must blend or be harmonious with that of their community, otherwise stagnation and self-absorption will prevent this from happening. The result will be alienation from community and a hiatus between self and community.[48]

Don Browning has also made some valuable and insightful contributions to our understanding of the concept of generativity by means of his book, *Generative Man.* He says:

> Generativity, for Erikson, is a process that stretches from man's most archaic and unconscious biological tendencies to the highest products of his imagination and his reason. . . . Generativity, not just libidinal sexuality, is the true archaic foundation of man. Certainly for Erikson, man is a creature of desire, but desire for him is more than sexual release or sensual enjoyment. Desire is a complex coordination of a wide range of instinctive patterns which all aim toward self-expression and self-confirmation through generativity.... Erikson refers to generativity as the instinctual power behind various forms of selfless caring.[49]

Stage Eight: *Integrity vs. Despair*

Erikson explains integrity as "the acceptance of one's own and only life cycle and of the people who have become significant to it as something that had to be and that, by necessity, permitted of no substitutions."

The person who has achieved integrity is also able to love his parents in ways that he did not experience before and to accept them in their totality. He is also able to accept the fact that the individual's life is his responsibility. Furthermore, the individual who has integrity views his life as something that has dignity, and as a life that is worthy of defense against any kind of threat.

In the lives of individuals whose ego integrity is absent and a fear of death is experienced, the matrix of this fear is despair.

> Despair expresses the feeling that the time is now
> short, too short for the attempt to start another
> life and to try out alternate roads to integrity.[50]

Many times despair of this nature is obscured by a show of disgust, misanthropy, or an expression of displeasure in institutions and people. The displeasure in institutions may be real and appropriate. However, this kind of behavior is an expression of the person's disgust with himself. Ego integrity implies that the person has achieved a level of degree of emotional integration which allows him to be a part of the next generation by being a follower of their leaders as well as to accept that responsibility which is part of leadership.

In his theory, Erikson has made some adjustments to Freud's point of view. He has given new meaning to Freud's psychoanalytic concepts and in this way he has "demythologized" and has given greater clarity as well as actuality to many of the psychoanalytical concepts used by Freud.[51] The term oedipal complex is a good example of this shift. Erikson says that "in its habitual connotations it is only the infantile and often only neurotic core of an existential dilemma which (less mythologically) may be called the generational complex, for it derives... generations."[52] In his theory of human development, Erikson's implicit ethic can be clearly discerned. This ethic comes out particularly clearly in his description and explanation of the way in which the human being passes through eight crucial stages and the way in which basic ego strengths or virtues evolve out of the resolution of the conflicts between opposing senses found in each stage. A propensity for ethics evolves in the human as it develops and Erikson sees this as an adaptational function of the individual.[53]

The ego of the individual plays an important role in its propensity for ethics. Browning says that the healthy ego does not seek its own good but that of the entire human race. As Erikson believes that the well-being and maintenance of the human race can only be done by means of generativity, and as generativity depends largely on a healthy ego, it is important to understand the ego in terms of its epigenesis, virtues, and rituals. For Erikson, the ego is the seat of ethics. These ethics are closely related to the ego with its developmental or epigenetic history which evolves over a period of time. However, it is only in adolescence that this ethical stage really takes root but it really only matures in middle and late adulthood. At the same time the important role of the prior stages of childhood and their importance for the development of an ethical sense in the individual must be overlooked.

Browning says that virtue is the end of ethical action--to create virtue in others and to enhance virtue in oneself.[54] The schedule of virtues that Erikson presents to us in his stage theory may act as good "guideposts" for *moral action* for individuals as well as institutions. A moral person who acts morally on the basis of a healthy ego as well as moral institutions always fills the person for whom it cares with strength and virtue. Simultaneously he builds up strength within himself. Erikson calls this mutual activation and regulation. Erikson also believes that the ego with its epigenetic nature is always affected by society, culture, and history. The healthy ego's aim is to improve constantly rituals or patterns that bring about mutual regulation and activation. These rituals form the fulcrum of a culture. And, culture, in turn, is a "complicated pattern (or ritual) of mutual activation and regulation."[55]

Generativity, like all the other positive virtues, is the product of a developmental synthesis which is in a cogwheeling relationship with the synthesis of previous stages in Erikson's theory of the life cycle. Every person needs this synthesis on the psychosocial level. If it does not take place, *fixation* occurs and even regression, e.g., the individual who does not experience synthesis in the generativity/stagnation stage will experience stagnation or self-absorption. When there is a successful synthesis of the poles of generativity and stagnation the virtue of *care* will be the result at this stage. The core of generativity is a deep capacity for care. In his interpretation of modernity, Erikson says that it is characterized by a nongenerative mentality or an inability to care for that which it creates or generates.[56]

It is interesting to note that there is an affinity between Erikson's ethics of recognition and Buber's "I-Thou" philosophy. We say "ethics of recognition" because Erikson's theory places great emphasis on the search for the face. This, for example, was part of the gift of Young Man Luther's struggle. He was searching for a face that he could recognize because in such a discovery lay his gifts of theological generativity. However, Erikson does not merely regard the "I-Thou" relationship as mere duality as is the case with Martin Buber.[57]

Erikson sees this relationship as contact between the adult and child of another individual with his adult and child. This for him is mutual recognition. To him this kind of relationship is of paramount importance for the "validation and preservation of individuals in the context of the generations."[58] For him it also has to do with the evolvement and the maintenance of the "strength" of human beings.

In his most recent publication, entitled *Outliving the Self*, John Kotre has given more body and broader meaning to Erikson's concept of generativity. The subheading of this book is "Generativity and the Interpretation of Lives." Kotre believes that Erikson's description of generativity fails to take into consideration the fact that there is a dark side to this concept, namely that it could lead to perversion. To illustrate this point he refers to Erikson's analysis of the lives of Gandhi and Luther as examples of this.

At the point of disagreement with Erikson, Kotre says in the light of the above it is impossible to view generativity exclusively as a virtue. In his modified view of generativity he defines it as:

> a desire to invest one's substance in forms of life
> and work that will outlive the self.[59]

According to Kotre, Erikson has brought an element of fixedness into his theory. One cannot limit generativity to virtuous expression or to a particular stage of the human life cycle, for example generativity can already be detected in the elements of care in child's play as it is expressed toward children who are younger than those in their age group. This is a valid point as it is clear to the observant student of Erikson's theory that generativity or elements of generativity do run through all the stages like a common golden thread. Erikson is aware of this however.

Kotre goes a little further than Erikson by delineating generativity into four major types. Another major critique that he has against Erikson is that the latter has failed to delineate these different types, namely: 1) Biological, 2) Parental, 3) Technical, 4) Cultural. Kotre describes these types as follows:

1) *Biological*: This encompasses fertility as it is explained by demographers. It refers to the begetting, production, and the care of children. The newborn baby is the focus of biological generativity. "Only in biological

transmission is material substance passed from the body of the progenitor to that of the creation."[60]

2) *Parental*: This is illustrated by the way in which the parent feeds, clothes, shelters, loves, and disciplines the child and guides it in the ways of the family. In Erikson's theory, such parental generativity brings about trust, autonomy, and initiative in the child.

3) *Technical*: The vehicle for this kind of generativity are teachers (not only professional) who convey skills to others who are still developing in life, e.g., reading skills, musical skills, skills to cope with the strains and stresses of life, etc. This kind of generativity occurs at various times between young adulthood and old age.

4) *Cultural*: this type of generativity involves the mind.

> When a teacher turns from how to do it to what it means, when she speaks of the idea of music or healing or law, when she brings to the fore the symbol system that stood in the background and offers the student the outlines of an identity, she becomes culturally generative. She is no longer a teacher of skills but a mentor, and her apprentice has become a disciple.[61]

Each of these types of generativity has a particular generative object as its focus as follows. In the case of the biological, the object is the infant. In the case of the parental, the generative object is the child.
In the case of the technical, the generative object is the apprentice and the skill. In the case of the cultural, the generative object is the disciple and the culture.

Modes of Generativity
In the expression of the types of generativity mentioned above, the progenitor may focus his life interest on himself or on the object of generativity. This is where the following two terms, namely "agentic mode" and

"communal mode," come into play. The agentic mode of generativity refers to a focusing of life interests on the progenitor. The communal mode occurs when life interests are focused on the generative object. These terms were first used by David Baken, a psychologist, to describe contradictory poles in the endeavor of human beings. Agency also represents self-assertion, self-protection, and self-expansion in the existence of an individual. Communion represents the participation of the individual in a mutual, interpersonal reality or in some larger organism.[62]

Virtues

Another major part of Erik Erikson's Life Cycle Theory is his discussion of virtues. Erikson believes that human strength must be viewed as "inherent strength." However he prefers to use the term "virtues" for:

> In Latin virtue meant virility, which at least suggests the combination of strength, restraint, and courage.... But old English gave a special meaning to the word "virtue" which does admirably. It meant inherent strength or active quality, and was used, for example, for the undiminished potency of well-preserved medicines and liquors....I will call "virtue," then, certain human qualities of strength, and I will relate them to that process by which ego strength may be developed from stage to stage and imparted from generation to generation.[63]

For humans to survive psychosocially certain virtues must be present. These virtues develop as generations succeed and overlap each other. Erikson uses a very fitting word for describing this overlapping as a "cogwheeling" of the life stages of one individual with another. By this he means that a person's life stages influence those of others and vice versa. Erikson therefore sees the human cycle as "an integrated social phenomenon."[64]

The virtues that Erikson has in mind are the following: hope, will, purpose, and competence (virtues developed in childhood); fidelity (adolescent virtue); and love, care, and wisdom (central virtues of adulthood). These virtues are all interdependent, e.g., there cannot be a form of reciprocal love until there is proof that fidelity is reliable. Will can only evolve when hope is on a secure foundation.

1. *Hope*: this is the earliest virtue and it is essential for the state of being alive. Erikson uses the example of the infant whose smile instills hope in the adult as well as a wish to impart hope to others. The infant thus brings about the strength in a mutual experience. According to Erikson the matrix of hope is trustworthy maternal persons who provide certain needs, e.g., warmth and food. The foundation of hope is thus provided by the infant's first love object, that is, the mother who provides it with the basic physical and emotional needs. This hope will mature as the infant develops. It will evolve into faith in the adult stage. Erikson says further:

> Hope is the enduring belief in the attainability of fervent wishes, in spite of the dark urges and rages which mark the beginnings of existence.[65]

2. *Will*: This does not refer to willfulness. By will, Erikson means the achieving of greater judgment and decisiveness in applying drives. Will evolves more and more in the individual as the ego integrates certain experiences, e.g., the training of a child in the use of its sphincters could become the focal point of the struggle of inner and outer control over each other which is located in the muscle system. The child will experience shame and doubt if it feels defeat due to inadequate training. On the other hand, however, will could be a powerful force in the personality if it receives a firm grounding in the early stages of the development of the ego.

This will contribute or enable the person to gain a knowledge of expectations that are placed on him by others and vice versa. Erikson says:

> Will, therefore, is the unbroken determination to exercise free choice as well as self-restraint, in spite of the unavoidable experience of shame and doubt in infancy.[66]

In the second and third year of the child's life the parents play a vital role in conveying a sense of justice to the child. The parents have the responsibility to instill in the young child the fact that in order to receive good will from other people it should place limitations on its own will on a mutual basis. The child learns that there are social boundaries that exist, which in turn indicate the presence or existence of limitations. The importance of this parental duty is based on the fact during these years (2-3 years) the child's world has expanded to include newcomers to whom it must now yield. The judicious parent now has to execute the vital function of respecting the privileges of the strong while at the same time protecting the weak with the rights that they have.

The child who learns to control willfulness offers willingness and lends good will to others. He will thus be rewarded by the parent with a certain degree of self-control. In all of the above the example set by the parent is of vital importance to the developing child. It should be an example that shows that they have autonomy which enables them to be masters of their own modalities. This example will encourage the child to develop a sense of independence and to make choices concerning its future. Broadly put, this will enable the child to have a positive self-image which has a healthy virtue of will which in turn makes the adult a responsible person. A person who possesses the virtue of will knows how to act with restraint as far as his own powers are concerned.

3. *Purpose*: Purpose is "a temporal perspective giving direction and focus to concerted striving." This develops in the child's play and fantasies. In his play the child learns what the purpose is of certain things. The family as a primary group plays an important role in demarcating for the child the boundaries between play and purpose. This is very important to the child, particularly when he becomes engaged in focusing on goals outside of the parameters of the family. It is also in the family that the child will internalize the prohibitions, encouragements, norms, and values of adults which help it to form a conscience. This in turn will enable the child to pursue certain goals in life which could be attained and those that could be shared. "Purpose, then, is the courage to envisage and pursue . . . punishment."[67]

4. *Competence*: Competence later becomes workmanship as the child develops. The child needs to learn to work as his intellectual and mental faculties develop. The school as a societal institution plays a vital role in developing the virtue of competence in the child. Here the child is taught to "work" and to become competent by using its mind and to be physically coordinated. This in turn enables the child to exercise certain skills and to achieve certain goals. The strengthening of its ability to use grammar and math, etc., further equips the child for work and workmanship in the future. Where this is absent the child will suffer from a weak ego and an inferiority complex. In a wider context, the virtue of competence helps the child to adapt better to its culture and not to be alienated from it. "Competence, then, is the free exercise of dexterity and intelligence in the completion of tasks, unimpaired by infantile inferiority."[68]

Furthermore, competence involves participation in a productive situation, usually in company with others. These others include peers who cooperate with him as well as instructive adults. At each stage of the life cycle the individual gains something developmentally. Competence is such a gain. It enables him to understand those materials that are basic to technology as well as the elements of reasoning by which it becomes possible for him to be taught those techniques he will need in order to be competent.

5. *Fidelity*: Fidelity is the ability to sustain loyalties freely pledged in spite of the inevitable contradictions of value systems. It is the cornerstone of identity and receives inspiration from confirming ideologies and affirming companions. Without a sense of fidelity youth cannot have an identity. To assist them to uphold this virtue of fidelity youth receive help in the form of adults who confirm them and peers who affirm them. Young people are always ready to pledge their loyalties to that which feels true and right to them. Erikson stresses that while identity and fidelity are the imperative elements of ethical strength, it is not provided by these but by adults. The basis for the adult virtues are completed when the young person chooses those who will choose him into their circle of friends, co-workers, etc. Those groups help to give him an identity and he will pledge his fidelity to them.

Erikson stresses that identity and fidelity are important elements that must be present if ethical strength is to evolve in the developing youth. However, these elements do not provide this ethical strength in themselves. It is the adult who must guide the loyalties which youth want to pledge. The adult must also provide youth with worthy objects which they can use to fulfill their need for repudiation.

6. *Love*:

> Love then is the mutuality of devotion forever subduing the antagonisms inherent in divided function.[69]

The above quotation suggests that love is an intimacy that develops with the conscious awareness of a man and a woman. This mutual devotion is a selfless commitment based on a foundation of mutuality. There is thus a mutual concern that develops between two people, a mutual concern for the caring of offspring, products, and ideas. This love also subdues differences between two people of the opposite sex and further brings about mutuality of functions. This love furthermore arises where two people take chances with their identities, that is, they risk the identity that they were seeking and found and fuse it with that of another person resulting in a combined identity. This virtue of love is a virtue that moves beyond self-satisfaction to care and concern for the other person. The virtue of love will only emerge fully when the individual is confident with his identity.

7. *Care*: Erikson defines care as the "widening concern for what has been generated by love, necessity, or accident; it overcomes the ambivalence adhering to irreversible obligation."[70]

The virtue of care arises in the adult stage of generativity vs. stagnation. For Erikson, generativity and care are inseparably connected. To care means to be responsible for what one creates. In talking about generativity Erikson is primarily focusing on the care of children by adults, care for that which they had generated or created. However, he says that the adult must also assume responsibility for other things which he creates like ideas and works.

Erikson refers to the person who does not care as experiencing stagnation or self-absorption. This also means that such an adult is practicing a kind of rejection of that to which he is supposed to be generative. Narcissism or preoccupation with the self is an example of stagnation or an attitude of not caring in some modern /present-day adults. By caring for a child the adult also helps to impart meaning to the developmental world of the child. He gives the child a "particular world image and a style of fellowship." In this caring context the adult transmits hope, will, purpose, and competence to the child which will help it to mature into a psychologically balanced adult.

Another aspect of caring is to teach those for whom the adult is responsible, e.g., the teaching of values that are important for the psychosocial well-being of the next generation. Erikson focuses on the strong relationship between caring and generativity by referring to generativity as "the instinctual power behind various forms of selfless caring" that "potentially extends to whatever a man generates and leave behind, creates, and produces or helps to produce."[71]

8. *Wisdom*: Erikson says that in old age the individual life cycle goes back to the place where it began. Old people go back to a "child-likeness seasoned with wisdom...." They may also become childish but wisdom makes the difference.

> Wisdom, then, is detached concern with life itself, in the face of death itself. It maintains and conveys the integrity of experience, in spite of the decline of bodily and mental functions. It responds to the need of the oncoming generation for an integrated heritage and yet remains aware of the relativity of all knowledge.[72]

The virtue of wisdom also refers to the fact that there are certain people who possess the ability to view the problems of humanity as a whole. In this way they bear testimony with their lives "of the closure of a style of life to the ensuing generation." This is what Erikson means by integrity, an integrity which can eliminate the despair of feeling spent and helpless.

Epigenesis
Erikson also explains the growth of the personality in terms of the Epigenetic Principle. This principle is derived from the growth of organisms in utero.

...this principle states that anything that grows
has a ground plan, and that out of this ground
plan the parts arise, each part having its time of
special ascendancy, until all parts have arisen to
form a functioning whole.[73]

If we take stage one of Erikson's theory as an
example we could explain it as follows in terms of the
epigenetic principle. If psychosocial adaptation is to occur
in the individual then there must be a favorable ratio of
basic trust over basic mistrust. However, at each stage
there is a critical period, a turning point or crisis. The
stage of basic trust vs. basic mistrust, which has been there
since the beginning in some form in the infant, comes to its
ascendence, meets its developmental crisis, and finds a
permanent solution, e.g., trust outweighing
mistrust--resulting in the evolvement of the virtue of hope.

The epigenetic principle is inseparably linked to the
psychosocial environment in which a particular personality
develops. Thus, an unhealthy environment can retard
growth at a given stage while a healthy environment will
foster growth.

Discussion Between Wright and Browning

Don Browning regards generativity as the normative
center of Erikson's thought. He also refers to generativity
as "the grand final synthesis of all the stages."[74] Wright
rejects this for two reasons, namely, in his opinion, the
"grand final synthesis" is a combination of mutuality and
generativity. He states furthermore that the Golden Rule
that forms the basis of Erikson's ethics incorporates both
mutuality and generativity. Wright opposes the idea of
isolating one particular point as the norm of Erikson's
thinking. He believes that this downplays the others. He
says:

> It is true that some strengths and some virtues
> are highlighted by Erikson as more basic, and
> thereby of greater significance than others. But
> the cycle in its very interaction is skewed when
> the balance is lost by making one element
> "normative" for all the rest.[75]

It is evident that Wright is expressing some valid opinions
but, on the other hand, he may be judging Browning too
harshly. It does not appear that Browning is deliberately
trying to do a "disservice to the remaining elements of an
intricately and determinedly holistic system" by
emphasizing generativity as being normative to Erikson's
theory.[76] Browning seems to imply instead that there is a
common thread of generativity or deep caring love (my
words) that runs through all the eight stages, reinforcing
them like a strong spinal cord. It is not evident that
Browning is merely taking one stage, namely generativity,
into focus while excluding the rest. His broader implication
comes through clearly, namely, that there is a strong
element of generativity in each of the eight stages.

However, if both of these interpreters of Erikson's
theory are correct or partially correct, then their thoughts
have serious implications for the makeup of the
personalities of black adults in South Africa. This will be
explained in greater detail in a later chapter. Furthermore,
Eugene Wright stresses a combination of mutuality and
generativity. But on the other hand, it seems that basically
he is not far from what Browning is saying, namely, that
mutuality and love are synonymous. And if love is
expressed in Erikson's use of the word *care* (the virue) then
everything boils down to the fact that Wright has no
argument with Browning. They are saying the same thing
from different perspectives.

CHAPTER 2

H. RICHARD NIEBUHR'S ETHICS OF RESPONSIBILITY

The core of H. Richard Niebuhr's work as a theologian is located in the field of ethics, where he reflects critically on the moral life of the person. For the purpose of this book, I will focus on *The Responsible Self.* The main focus of this chapter will therefore be on this piece of literature. For H. Richard Niebuhr, reflection on the moral life is intricately interwoven with Christian theology. Therefore it is important not to divorce his ethics from the structure of his theology.

It is not my intention to make a critical and intensive study of the whole scope of Niebuhr's theology, as that is beyond the limitations of this book. The focus of this chapter will be on Niebuhr's Ethics of Responsibility. Later we shall view this in a relationship with Erik Erikson's concept of adulthood and generativity. Therefore, Niebuhr's concept or symbol of the Responsible Self will be dealt with in depth as I want to employ it and Niebuhr's ethical theory of responsibility together with Erikson's psychosocial theory to enable black adults in South Africa to be engaged in more effective self-analysis and self-understanding. This method could also aid them in making a more accurate evaluation of their moral dilemma. More specifically, we want to gain a better understanding of the moral behavior and actions of black South Africans as responsive and responsible beings in a society that limits their ability to execute their ethical responsibilities.

A Brief Description of the Structure of Niebuhr's Theology

In order to interpret Niebuhr's theological structure it is helpful to refer to some of the theological thoughts of Jonathan Edwards.[1] Libertus Hoedemaker[2] believes that there is an affinity between some of the themes of Edwards and Niebuhr, e.g., those dealing with God as the great system of being which is the source of value for all beings;

the Sovereignty of God; and the Center of ethics as the love of being.

Strongly associated with revivalism in the 18th century, Edwards was concerned with changes that were occurring at that time. These changes influenced the faith of the people and their relationship to God, e.g., increasing rationalism, etc. Such factors caused Edwards to build the framework of the Divine Sovereignty. He stressed the fact that human beings could only fully comprehend the dynamics of the various situations they find themselves in when it is seen in the light of the sovereignty of God. This formed the core of his thinking, which alone (for him) could explain human behavior.

H. Richard Niebuhr was deeply concerned about the problem of how people interpreted actions upon them which affected their behavior. Like Edwards, he wanted to rediscover the power of theocentric thinking as a means of understanding and interpreting human behavior. This fact comes out more clearly in his work particularly after the period of the publication of his *Kingdom of God in America.*[3] This prompted Hoedemaker to say:

> Perhaps the rediscovery of Jonathan Edwards is for Niebuhr one of the aspects of rediscovery of God....God who was caught in the chains of benevolence and immanence and whose sovereignty is now restored....[4]

Niebuhr recognizes his own concerns, particularly for a link between God's sovereignty and human action and hope in the theological thoughts and framework of Edwards. The major themes that run through H. Richard Niebuhr's theological structure are the themes of *monotheism* and *transformation.*

> Monotheism--a consistent concentration on the one God--implies transformation: all human thought and social expression must engage itself

in a constant process of redirection toward the
one God.[5]

The concept of monotheistic faith means that God is one.
This one God is the only God. It also means love of being
and to respond to the challenge that is presented to us in
the cause of God. There can be monotheistic faith only if
this faith can fully believe that the one God is good.[6] The
important question that comes to us though is how far we
are able to respond to God who is the goodness of being in
all our actions. This question places the emphasis on the
faith of the individual.

Niebuhr believes that there can only be true
response to God's actions and his presence when the person
has appropriated *insight* about it and (interprets it
correctly). Niebuhr says further that all of life is
characterized by responsiveness. This thought is brought
out very clearly in his book *The Responsible Self.*[7] In this
book he uses the symbol of the responsible man or man-the-
answerer/Homo Dialogicus. It is important to take a closer
look at this book as it gives this chapter its major emphasis.

The Responsible Self is Niebuhr's critical inquiry
"into the nature of the moral life (of a community), the
principles of its life...."[8] This inquiry he does through the
universal moral theme of responsibility. It brings into play
the relationships of people to God and the interrelationships
of people before God. Niebuhr sees his task, namely, as
that of a critical inquiry into the moral life, as that of the
analysis of "ethos" and to lay bare the roots of and
fundamental character of a community's moral life. In other
words, one could say that it is a moral inquiry that leads to
self-analysis by the individual members of a community and
self-knowledge which is of paramount importance to the
responsible life. Niebuhr is careful not to extend the claims
of Christian ethics too far and places certain limitations on
it. He is careful not to convey the impression that Christian
ethics is morally superior to that of the non-Christian. He

says, "the proper stance of the Christian community in its ethical reflection is self-criticism and repentance, not pride and aggrandizement."[9]

The Meaning of Responsibility

The "theory of responsibility" was developed by H. Richard Niebuhr to give us a more appropriate way to view morality. He was aware of the existence of other theories, though, e.g., deontological and teleological theories. While he believed that the latter two are helpful to us in our interpretation of moral action, they had deficiencies that had to be overcome. For him, the symbol of "responsibility" gave people an alternate way to view their moral lives. Not only is it more adequate than the above theories, but it also goes beyond their inherent limitations. Niebuhr said:

> Our task rather is to try with the aid of this symbol to further the double purpose of ethics: to obey the ancient and perennial commandment, "Gnothi Seauton," "Know Thyself," and to seek guidance for our activity as we decide, choose, commit ourselves, and otherwise bear the burden of our necessary human freedom.[10]

People are agents, says Niebuhr which means that they are beings who are in charge of their conduct.[11] As agents people have always wanted to gain better self-knowledge. Therefore they employ two important symbols to do so, namely, the symbol of the maker, *Homo Faber*, and the symbol of the citizen or the person living under the law, *Homo Politicus*.

The symbol of the maker suggests that in their actions people are like skilled craftsmen and women who create things with a specific end goal in mind. Human moral action has been viewed in this way too. When the individuals act in the above way they are acting teleologically with a telos or goal in mind. William

Frankena takes the idea of the telos a little further, when he says:

> A teleological theory says...an act is right if and only if it or the rule under which it falls produces, will probably produce, or is intended to produce at least as great a balance of good over evil as any available alternative; an act is wrong only if it does not do so.[12]

This suggests that teleological action strives for the highest good in people.

The symbol of the *citizen* gives us a picture of a person living under the law. The reality of our moral existence can also be interpreted by means of this symbol. No human life can be lived outside the gambit of some law or another whether it is the laws of primitive man or the prohibitions of parents to children.[13] There is no doubt that the symbol of the citizen can be applied to our moral lives and actions especially when we ask or are forced to ask in different situations:

> To what law shall I consent, against what law rebel? By what law or system of laws shall I govern myself and others? How shall I administer the domain of which I am the ruler or in which I particate to rule?[14]

But to Niebuhr it is not good enough for the accurate interpretation of the moral life because it does not answer among others the crucial question: What is this law doing to me as a person? To my selfworth? To my being? To my personality? However we cannot deny that this symbol which enables the self to conceive of itself as a legislative agent is useful to some extent and does help us in the making of difficult decisions as:

>...we come into being under the rules of family,
>neighborhood, and nation, subject to the
>regulation of our action by others.[15]

When people try to interpret their moral lives from a
legislative point of view then they are acting deontologically.
Deontology always wants to know first what the law is all
about and what the first law of the person's life is.[16] In
stark contrast to the above two symbols and theories, the
symbol of the Responsible Man always causes the person to
ask: What is going on?" Such a question is asked when an
individual is faced with decisions and choices.   To this
symbol we shall now turn.

The Symbol of Responsibility

The prominent role that the person plays in this
kind of symbolism is that of answerer (*Homo Dialogicus*).
The person responds to actions upon him.   Answering,
however, is only part of all the actions of a person.   But
with the aid of this symbolism, Niebuhr wants to show that
all of the actions of a person can be patterned after an
answering response in the context of a dialogue:

>An now we try to think of all our actions as
>having the character of being, responses, answers
>to actions upon us.[17]

This type of response, however, depends on the way
in which the responder *interprets* the actions upon him.
The important role of interpretation is clearly illustrated
when the person has to respond to suffering. It is precisely
within the context of suffering that the validity of Niebuhr's
symbol of Responsibility is seen especially when we place
this image alongside the images of "man-the-maker" and
"man-the-citizen." In a situation of suffering the sufferer is
not interested in the goal of suffering (cf. Teleological theory
and the image of "man-the-maker"), neither is the person

interested in the legal aspects of suffering (cf. Deontological theory) or "man-the-citizen." In a situation of suffering a choice or decision has to be made to terminate or eliminate the suffering. Therefore, the responsible person responds almost instinctively by asking, "What is happening to me?" or "What is going on?"

There are four elements or assumptions that are basic to the theory of responsibility, by which it can be analyzed, namely:
1) response, 2) interpretation, 3) accountability, and 4) social solidarity.

1. *Response*

Response is the first element in the theory of responsibility. It is important to differentiate between response and reaction. Knee jerks and heartbeats are reactions. Moral action is response to action upon us guided by our interpretation of such action. Response occurs when the element of interpretation is present.[18]

2. *Interpretation*

The second element in the theory of responsibility has to do with the way the individual interprets things. Interpretation leads to a certain kind of response. Interpretation comes about when the individual wants to know what is happening to him.

3. *Accountability*

When a person responds he expects other individuals in his environment to object to, confirm, or correct that response.[19] With every response that the individual makes he must take into account that he can expect reactions to it. Jerry Irish put it nicely:

> Accountability is another way of posing the question: "To whom or what am I responding and in what context?" When responsibility theory is used as an instrument of analysis, accountability

identifies the self's expectations of reactions to its
own responses and the sense of judgment implied
in that expectation.[20]

4. *Social Solidarity*

The fourth element in the theory of responsibility is
social solidarity. Niebuhr says:

> Our action is responsible, it appears, when it is
> response to action upon us in a continuing
> discourse or interaction among beings forming a
> continuing society.[21]

Social solidarity means that a person has a continuing and
consistent relationship in a given community. The
responsible self in a context of social solidarity therefore
acts with a connectedness in being. By this is meant a self
that is connected to society and a self that is in time. It is
also a self with a sense of absolute dependence and a self
that is part of a whole.[22]

One of the most crucial aspects of Niebuhr's
responsibility theory for this book is the fact that it presents
us with an important *key* for understanding the biblical
ethos which will in turn inform my biblical approach to
pastoral counseling which will be described in more detail
in the last chapter. There have been attempts in the past
to try to understand this ethos teleologically as well as
deontologically.   Barth and Bultmann, for example,
regarded the ethics of the Bible as the ethics of *obedience* or
in a deontological fashion.[23] Niebuhr disagrees with them
and believes that the symbolism of responsibility offers the
best tool for the critical analysis of the biblical ethos. While
this theory does not give the whole answer, almost
everything in the Bible could be understood by means of the
idea of responsibility, according to Niebuhr. At critical
stages in Israel's history in the Old Testament, "the decisive

question men raised was not: What is the goal? nor yet What is the law? but What is happening?" and then "What is the fitting response to what is happening?"[24]

Niebuhr uses Isaiah chapter 10 as a classical example to explain how appropriate the theory of responsibility is for interpreting the biblical ethos. It is a fitting paradigm of the ethics of response to divine action. In this chapter the people of Israel are faced with a dangerous dilemma, namely the invasion by Assyria. There were many ways to respond, but which was the fitting one-- a teleological or a deontological response?

Isaiah first interprets the situation for the people. He asks them to see the divine purpose behind the event /dilemma which is in stark contrast to that of the Assyrians. His counsel to the people is that their response to the situation should be focused on God's infinite intention. In other words, they should be asking: "What is God doing?" That is the primary question. The response that will evolve from such a question would lead to responsibility to God.

Niebuhr agrees that to analyze biblical ethics with the image of responsibility is not a unique way for the comprehension of our ethical lives, but it does assist us in interpreting some of the dynamics that are at play in our lives better than deontological and teleological theories are able to do. It is helpful for the further understanding of the responsibility theory to compare it once again to deontological theory which says: "We ought to be responsible."

Niebuhr draws clear lines of demarcation between the understanding of responsibility as a conceptual scheme for understanding morality and the way obligation does. He states clearly that morality, all morality, grows out of interpretation of our existence. Morality does not evolve due to response to an ought. When this view is taken then we link the evolvement of morality to laws. This is what Barth is guilty of doing. Due to the great emphasis that he placed on the sovereignty of God, Barth said that because

God is sovereign therefore we *ought* to....But in the end, Barth is forced to concede that there is disharmony between God's sovereignty and obligation (deontology). The implication of this is that for people, God's will can be opposed in that people could do what they are obliged to rather than being responsible to it.[25]

The Self in the Conceptual Scheme of Responsibility

The self is central to the understanding of the responsibility theory. Therefore, Niebuhr's understanding or definition of self should be clearly defined in order to be able to understand fully how such a self comes into being and responds to actions upon it. Niebuhr stresses the fact that the self is social. By this he means that self can only know itself in relation to other selves. This self can only exist in relation to or in response to other selves. This understanding of the self he derives from social psychology and more specifically from the thoughts of George Herbert Mead and Martin Buber. Mead says that the self is its own object due to the fact that it is in a situation of dialogue with other selves.

> To be a being that is an object to itself is possible genetically and actually only as I take toward myself the attitude of other selves, see myself as seen, hear myself as heard, speak to myself as spoken to.[26]

For a clear understanding of Niebuhr's use of self it would be helpful to refer briefly to the two sources who helped him to formulate such an understanding, namely, Mead and Buber. George Herbert Mead was an American philosopher and social psychologist and a pragmatist of the "Chicago School." According to him:

> The Self arises where the individual form has the ability to take the attitude of the group to which he belongs, then to come back upon himself, stimulate himself as he stimulates others, talk to himself in terms of his community, and lay upon himself the responsibilities that go with the community life.[27]

This selfhood evolves with the aid of language symbols to become a "socius" or an object to itself by taking the attitude and roles of others upon him/herself. That is why an infant cannot be described as a self. The reason being that it cannot yet separate itself from its own perceptions. The child is subject to the perceptions that he has as he organizes the physical world that surrounds him.

> From observing the play of children Mead came to believe that it is when a child is able in his play to assume different roles that he becomes aware of himself and of others in the mutual relations of social interaction. The continuing expansion and enrichment of the personality follows the same process. The child will not succeed in forming an object of himself--of putting the so-called subjective material of consciousness within such a self--until he has recognized about him social objects which have arisen in his experience.[28]

The child is firmly embedded in his perceptions. Only when he becomes individuated from them does he become a self (by using language, by being able to see himself as object, etc.).[29] This leads to responsibility. According to Mead the self "is in a social structure and its matrix is social experience."[30] The way in which he perceives himself and experiences himself is contributed by members of his social group. Both Mead and Erik Erikson emphasize the same key note, namely, that the self (Mead) or personality (Erikson) is not present at birth. It develops in a process of social experience. The importance of the role of the environment which involves other human beings in the formation of the self is thus clearly illustrated here. What comes out particularly clearly is the role of the environment in the process that eventually leads to the formation of responsibility and the formation of the moral self.

Lest it appear as if the evolvement of the self is being oversimplified, Mead mentions that this process may involve conflict as well, as any normal individual continually reacts against society as it asserts itself in search of recognition, etc.[31] Mead also mentions the importance of "the generalized other" whose role the individual self may also assume. By generalized other, Mead means the organized community which gives to the self a sense of unity and exerts a measure of control over it/him.[32] The generalized other is of special significance to Niebuhr. In his dynamic Triad of Faith, the generalized other is called "other selves."

At times Mead contradicts himself and makes himself guilty of not being very clear about the self's relationship to the "generalized other." He uses a term that seems to be more felicitous than empirically grounded. It is hard to believe that the individual should become a generalized other before becoming him/herself. Furthermore Mead's view that other selves antedate the consciousness of self is problematic.[33] This is possibly what Niebuhr had in mind with his use of the above concept.

The second person who helps Niebuhr in his understanding of the self is Martin Buber. Like Mead, Buber also sees man as a "socius" and also stresses the important role played by the relations between people. But both of them have different ways of approaching the problem of the social self.   Each have their own *weltanschauung*.   However, Buber stayed within an existential and religious orbit to evolve his concept of the self, while Mead works within a secular structure. Buber, therefore, can only be comprehended within a religious framework. He also writes from a faith perspective (The Jewish Chasidic Faith).

> His interest lies not even in God as a being who occupies a definite position in a definite system of thought, but in God as the reality whom man meets, and to whom man can respond.[34]

Buber, like Mead, stresses the fact that the individual becomes a self from within a *social matrix*-- through gesture and response and address and answer ....[35] By reflecting existentially, Buber arrives at the "I-Thou" and the "I-It" characteristics of the self. "I and Thou stand for Self and Other in the context of Buber's usage of these terms. Buber regards the encounter with the Thou as the key to the understanding of reality."[36] While Niebuhr acknowledges his indebtedness to Buber, his thoughts are closer to Mead, especially Mead's thoughts on the evolving of the self through other selves. Niebuhr believes in the relational existence of the self. He calls this kind of existence social existentialism.[37]

Social existentialism means further that the self is a being that only knows itself in relation to other selves and its only form of existence is in that relation. In its context of social existentialism the self finds self-actualization only when it is in a relationship to a Center of Value. In this case that center of value is God.

With this background information on Mead's and Buber's analyses of the self we now have to pay attention to what Niebuhr calls the Dynamic Triad of Faith in which the self is intricately involved. For Hoedemaker the central function of the triad of faith in Niebuhr's theological structure maintains that if there is to be any relevance to any speaking about God then such speaking must be built into the structure of the triad and must be reflected by it. In other words, what Hoedemaker is implying is that anything we say about God only takes on meaning when it is said in the context of God-self-neighbor and world. There is a close affinity and an interrelationship between all these.[38]

The triad of faith forms the most important factor in Niebuhr's way of analyzing self and community as being responsive and responsible. It also forms the basis for exploring social selfhood in Niebuhr's theological scheme. Niebuhr illustrates the triadic nature of situations where responsibility and responsivity occur in two ways. First, by means of a *nature triad* and second, by means of a *cause triad*.

In the natural triad the self has a dual relation to society or to social companions and to nature whereby natural events become known to us. This triad is also referred to as the I-Thou-Nature triad. Basic to this triad is a bond of trust that exists between the selves in this triad. By nature, Niebuhr refers to:

> ...that large world of events and agencies that we regard as impersonal, as purely objective or thing-like in character.[39]

In this triad there is a dialogue between three partners, namely, the self, the social companion, and natural events. The self also acts as a social self who responds to other selves in every response to nature. In this regard the self is a responsible self responding to nature and who has other selves reacting to it while they respond to the natural event as well.

In the other triad, Niebuhr says the self also responds and is responsible. The element, however, that is basic to this triad is that of *loyalty*. The person now responds by a loyalty and a commitment to a cause. In this commitment the self/person is linked to others who are also committed to the same cause, e.g., a patriot who is loyal to his/her country (cause) while being loyal to his/her fellow citizens at the same time. In this triadic structure the cause is always something personal on the one hand, while on the other hand, it is something that transcends the selves.

On a religious plane, the monotheistic believer responds to fellow believers in the church. The term monotheism will be explained in detail in a later subheading. At the same time, the believers are committed to each other as they respond to God, the ultimate cause. The triad points us to the fact that we all exist in a context of social relationships with other people by virtue of a cause/es.

> A cause, then, is truly an object of devotion, a god; To be a self is to have a god.[40]

Furthermore, it is faith that binds selves to each other and to their common cause--a faith that is built on trust and loyalty. In this regard, we should mention that Niebuhr owes the latter thoughts about cause and loyalty to Josiah Royce's philosophy. Royce believes that the moral self evolves on the basis of loyalty. Niebuhr believes firmly that the triadic structure of faith prevails in every relationship that the self finds itself in. The pinnacle of the triadic form of faith finds expression in a cosmic form in Jesus Christ. Niebuhr elaborates nicely on this in his article, "The Triad of Faith."[41] This cosmic form could be equated as God, the Self, and Neighbor (also called the theological and anthropological triad); God, man, and Christ (the christological triad); God, self, and being (the ethical triad).

The Interpretation of Moral Experience

Niebuhr basically uses two separate schemes to interpret the dynamics of our moral lives. On the one hand, we have the scheme that focuses on responsibility. While he replaces the center of value scheme in his later work with the responsibility scheme, the former still forms an intrinsic part of the latter. In fact, without a good comprehension of the former we cannot fully understand the dynamics of the latter, particularly insofar as it describes the intimate link between the social existence of human beings and their absolute dependence on the ultimate cause of reality (God).

The Center of Value

The thoughts that are expressed very broadly under this subheading are derived from what I learned from the supplementary essay, "The Center of Value," in Niebuhr's book *Radical Monotheism and Western Culture*.[42] I will not go into the finer details of this concept but will only give the main points here in broad outline to explain Niebuhr's understanding of the "Center of Value" in a coherent fashion.

According to Niebuhr, value theorists usually use a relational theory of value in their reflections of what is "good" by referring to a being for which other beings are good.[43] He says further that "Relational Value Theory agrees with objectivism on this further point, that what is good for man or for society or for any other being which represents the starting point of inquiry, is not determined by the desire of that being."[44] The points of a relational value theory are as follows, namely: We observe value when an existent being that possesses capacities and potentialities comes up against another that has a *limiting*, complementing, or completing effect on it. This means that an observer notices value when one being is fit or unfit for another. This in turn refers to the fact that one being may be positive or negative, good or evil to another. In this context good refers to that which meets the needs of a certain being and evil refers to that which "thwarts, destroys, or starves a being in its activities."[45] Relational value theory further refers to the fact that being and value are intimately related to each other. Niebuhr says further that:

> Value is present wherever being confronts being, wherever there is becoming in the midst of plural, interdependent, and interacting existences, It is not a function of being as such but of being in relation to being....For if anything existed simply in itself and by itself, value would not be present....This value is not a relation but arises in the relations of being to being.[46]

As good as the above may sound, we should not lose sight of the fact that while relational value theory does offer solutions to problems, and that while it is especially helpful to our understanding of the analysis of the structure of moral lives, it is also viewed with great suspicion by others, particularly those who are more concerned about right relations between people and between people and their physical and ecological environment.[47] In other words, people who hold these suspicions are more concerned with right relations between human beings and between human beings and their non-human environment.

Every value theory has a starting point grounded in a being/s who is/are seen as existing in a relationship with other beings "in relation to which good is judged to be good and evil, in relation to which also the rightness or wrongness of its relations to other beings is examined."[48] Therefore the starting point of a monotheistic faith is the transcendent, there is *one* "for whom alone there is an ultimate good and for whom, as the source and end of all things, whatever is, is good."[49]

The Schema of Responsibility

The point of departure for Niebuhr's schema of responsibility is the observation that all life has the character of responsiveness. He suggests further that the broad-based symbol of the responsible man might even give new relevance to Christ.

Of great importance in this schema is the dynamic triad of faith. Niebuhr says that the knowledge that the self acquires and the way in which it communicates with others have a triadic pattern. This is a central point in his responsibility schema. The self is constantly engaged in a dialogue that involves the self, the social companion, and natural events. This is the first of two triadic situations that he employs in his ethics. This first triad is also called the I-Thou-Nature triad.

The *a priori* element of covenant or commitment between selves, which involves trust, is a further important point in Niebuhr's thinking. According to him, there cannot be trust on an interpersonal basis unless a third, that is, an "it" is present. The conditioning of selfhood by the presence of other selves is what is of particular interest to Niebuhr.

The self also operates in a second triadic situation, namely, the I-Thou-Cause triad. In this case the cause is the third reality by means of which the self and other selves are linked. Hoedemaker puts it nicely:

> The cause sustains and feeds the relation; and a community--a more or less stable pattern of constant response and interpretation--can be a community only by virtue of such a common and binding cause. It makes interpersonal trust possible.[50]

He says further that a cause is an object of devotion, a god. "To be a self is to have a god."[51]

The triad of faith has a central function for Niebuhr. Any speaking about God must form an integral part of the triad and be a reflection of it if it is to have any meaning. This means that such speaking will only be meaningful if they involve statements about the interrelationship between the self, the neighbor, and the world. Because it is in such interpersonal processes that faith is always manifested.

In the responsibility schema Niebuhr uses the image of responsibility to give us a more vivid description of the self in action. Furthermore he uses this schema to show how every action and response of the self is response to God and how it always takes place in the midst of a field of forces which include other selves. He uses this schema to show how we experience and interpret the one divine action of God which happens to us.

This schema is also used to show that the only adequate response for man is when he responds to everything as if responding to the sovereign God with a radical monotheistic faith or with a fundamental trust in a God who is the ultimate cause of all things.

Why the Incorporation of the Center of Value Into the Responsibility Schema?

Niebuhr incorporated the concept of the Center of Value into the Responsibility Schema for various reasons, reasons that are harmonious with his way of viewing the responsible man. He looks at the way in which various value theorists, e.g., Nikolai Hartman, G. E. Moore, and Hume, deal with concrete ethical problems and then draws the following conclusions, that is:

> ...they usually employ a relational theory of value which defines good by reference to a being for which other beings are good.[52]

Niebuhr's interest, among others, is in situations in which the self as a social being is in the process of becoming itself who interacts with other selves as social beings.

In such situations or interrelationships value appears. But I must emphasize that Niebuhr wishes to present a theory of value that is social. This he does very adequately in the responsibility schema as he describes the social self responding to other social selves and to God who gives meaning to our responses in a dynamic triad of faith. Niebuhr says, "...the basis of this relational value theory is not the relation of existence to essence, it is that of self to other."

On a philosophical level, Niebuhr is more indebted to George Mead than to Aristotle for the basis of the relational value theory. On the theological level, he is more indebted to Jonathan Edwards than to Aquinas.[53] With the aid or incorporation of the Center of Value Theory the *Responsibility Schema* is made clearer and its adequacy comes out. The understanding of the self and the way it responds can only be understood in relation to a value center. For Niebuhr, and for every Christian, this Center of Value is God. He is the norm of all value. He is the transcendent One. He can only be grasped by a radical monotheistic faith.

This idea was expounded by George Herbert Mead and Niebuhr saw a lot of value in it for his ethical theory. But it is meant that the self organizes the responses that it makes on the basis of the responses that it expects others to make. In other words, when the self becomes an object to itself it is able to assume the role of other selves with whom it interacts. If we take this a step further we may say that such a self is perhaps in a better position to see and understand how God is acting on it. This is possibly what Niebuhr had in mind with his use of the above concept.

In his reflection on the predicament of modern man/woman and the way they respond to their predicaments and in his analysis of the self in its triadic form, Niebuhr finds that the problem of faith presents itself over and over again. We cannot do justice to Niebuhr's schema of responsibility without some discussion of faith as it is viewed by him, as well as the relationship of Christian faith to monotheism. For Niebuhr, theology and faith are intricately interwoven.

We now turn to such a discussion.

Faith

In his book, *Radical Monotheism and Western Culture*,[54] Niebuhr writes that in American culture there is a conflict of faiths which he sees as one between radical monotheism and other faiths, e.g., polytheism and henotheism. Hoedemaker refers to polytheism as the coexistence of many gods...and to henotheism as that type of faith which choose "one of the many objects of devotion and turns it into the only one."[55] Hoedemaker believes that henotheism is the more dangerous of the two. He writes further, "Henotheism is a social faith which makes a finite society, whether cultural or religious, the object of trust as well as of loyalty...which tends to subvert... monotheistic institutions, such as churches."[56]

Niebuhr characterizes faith as the "attitude and action of confidence in, and fidelity to, certain realities as the sources of value and the object of loyalty."[57] He also refers to faith as the trust we place in that which values the self.[58] And he cites nationalism as an example where people place so much faith in a nation that it becomes their center of value. Loyalty or fidelity go hand in hand with trust in a value center and further reinforces faith. When Niebuhr speaks about faith in his responsibility scheme he means specifically a radical monotheistic faith. This monotheism expresses its loyalty to "One beyond all the many." Subsequently it is in perpetual tension with a pluralistic faith that owes its allegiance to several objects of devotion and on the other hand, "a social faith that has one object...among many."[59]

The Concept of Radical Monotheism and its
Place in Niebuhr's Ethics

Radical monotheism is a form of faith. It has as its center of value the One who is beyond the many. From this One it obtains its being.

> As faith it is a reliance on the source of all being
> for the significance of the self and of all that
> exists. It is the assurance that because I am, *I*
> *am valued.*....It is the confidence that whatever is,
> is good because it exists as one thing among the
> many which all have their origin and their being,
> in the One--the principle of being which is also
> the principle of value.[60]

A very important fact that has far-reaching implications for this book is the point Niebuhr makes that monotheism cannot be radical if it draws lines of demarcation between the principle of being and the principle of value, "only some beings are valued as having worth for it."[61] This explains how self-worth is ascribed to or taken away from certain individuals in certain situations. It leads us to ask: "Do people who make themselves guilty of such practices have a radical monotheistic faith or is it just another form of henotheism?" This question is an important one for this book and it will be dealt with later. Niebuhr, however, answers this question to a certain degree by stating that in radical monotheism one's neighbor is one's companion in being. And even though I may regard my neighbor as an enemy it is expected of me to love that person.[62]

A critique which could be levelled at Niebuhr at this point is that in view of the latter thought his triad of faith seems to have a partially felicitous structure. Niebuhr does not make allowance for the *disruption* of the triad which can occur due to the fact that in the triadic scheme a distinction is sometimes made between principle of being and principle of value and the neighbor is not regarded as a companion in a context of love rendering the triad unworkable because the One beyond the many is dishonored by such action. In his book, *The Purpose of the Church and Its Ministry*,[63] Niebuhr in fact talks about that which could disrupt the triad but he does not accede to it. He says:

> The interrelations of self, companion, and God are so intricate that no member of this triad exists in his true nature without the others, nor can he be known or loved without the others... God's love of self and neighbor, neighbor's love of God and self, self's love of God and neighbor are so closely interrelated that none of the relations exist without the other.[64]

The above quotation reinforces that fact that radical monotheism is nonexistent where the neighbor is not valued as a being with worth before God, the Source and Center of all being, and that the triad thus becomes disrupted in this way. Niebuhr believes that the ultimate goal of the church and its *pastoral care* is the increase of love for God and neighbor, among people. This is where Niebuhr's theological structure places the Christian Church in South Africa and with its pastoral care and pastoral care implications in a serious dilemma, a crisis which can only be overcome if that church, in a spirit of humility and repentance and honesty before God defines for itself what its ultimate purpose is.

The love of God that Niebuhr refers to is not to be interpreted simplistically, but in relational terms. It is a rather complex issue but its understanding is made clear to us in the context of Niebuhr's schema of the dynamic triad of faith. Waldo Beach,[65] an interpreter of Niebuhr, says that the quality of love is determined by its directions. He understands love in terms of vertical and horizontal dimensions. In its vertical dimension love refers to its quality in terms of the relation of man to God in the way man honors God. This, says Beach, is epitomized in the

words of the New Testament: "You shall love the Lord your
God with all your heart, and with all your soul, and with all
your might." Beach says: "The horizontal dimension of love
means to cherish the whole created order, as the expression
of the love of God--and thy neighbor as thyself...." There is
no such thing as a love of God which does not in some way
entail love of neighbor, says Beach. He says further that we
would make ourselves guilty of distorting Christian ethics,
if we loved only God and excluded the neighbor. The God
that we communicate with on our knees is the one who after
such an act directs us to our neighbor to serve him/her and
to help to alleviate their needs.[66] It is our responsibility as
Christians to help our neighbor to find complete fulfillment
in God.[67] With the above thoughts, Beach is giving us a
triad of Christian love which is congruent with and also has
parallels with Niebuhr's triad of faith. Together these two
triads reinforce the responsiveness and responsibility of the
individual.

Jesus as our Model of Responsibility

We come now to the question: How do Christians
reflect on their moral lives as agents? Niebuhr says that in
their reflection on their moral life man/woman makes use of
symbols in order to understand the world in which they
interact better and to make it easier to grasp. Thus, in
Christianity, Jesus functions as a symbolic form which helps
us to understand God better:

> ...he is a form which they employ as an *a
> priori*, an image, a scheme or pattern in the
> mind which gives form and meaning to their
> experiences.[68]

Jesus as symbol influences the way that Christians as
agents judge, respond to, and make moral decisions,
understand themselves and guide their actions. It is

impossible to interpret the Christian moral life by divorcing it from the symbol of Jesus Christ. Niebuhr reminds us that Jesus is not the only symbol that Christians use and have used in the past to interpret their actions. To this Karl Barth takes strong exception. He is opposed to the inclusion of any analogy, metaphors, or symbols from Christian speech and action with the exception of Jesus Christ.[69] But Niebuhr makes it clear that this is impossible. He says that it is not possible to talk about Christian ethics without symbols like law, obedience, and commandment.[70] Christians have used these two metaphors together with the Christ symbol to interpret their moral lives, first, they have used the symbol of man-the-maker (*homo faber*) and second, man-the-citizen (*homo politicus*). But Niebuhr found these two symbols to be inadequate for the interpretation of our moral lives and therefore he proposed the symbol of the Responsible Self or man-the-responder (*homo dialogicus*) as an alternative and better way for interpreting the moral life.

When the focus is placed on Jesus in the context of Niebuhr's responsibility structure, it becomes evident that he interpreted or viewed every action on him as Divine Action or as coming directly from God. He gives us a few examples of the way in which Jesus interpreted actions upon him:

> He sees as others do that the sun shines on criminals, delinquents, hypocrites, honest men, good Samaritans, and V.I.P.s without discrimination, that rains come down in equal proportions on the fields of the diligent and the lazy. These phenomena have been for unbelief, from the beginning of time, signs of the operation of a universal order that is without justice, unconcerned with right and wrong among men. But Jesus interprets the common phenomena in another way: here are the signs of cosmic generosity....[71]

Niebuhr's thoughts on Jesus as the paradigm of responsibility are of special significance for this book in particular, because the way in which Jesus responded to actions on him that limited his responses and which were destructive to him in many ways sheds light on and is a good example of how people who experience situations that are similar to that should respond.   Jesus always interpreted every action on him by relating them to God.

> He responds to the infinite intention behind or inclusive of all the finite intentions.   He understands that Pilate would have no power over him had it not been granted to the procurator from above.[72]

The way in which Jesus interprets and responds to actions upon him in a Divine context reinforces and shows up the inadequacy of the theories of man-the-maker and man-the-citizen and also emphasizes the usefulness and actuality of Niebuhr's Responsibility theory for interpreting the moral life. Furthermore it means that we can take God seriously especially in our struggles to interpret our moral lives.   It also reemphasizes the validity of a radical monotheistic faith in the One beyond the many. This also says a lot for the ultimate goal of pastoral care, namely a goal of increase of love for God and neighbor. It says that by interpreting actions upon us in a divine context like Jesus did we will be enabled to trust God fully; to devote our loyalty to him and to be reconciled to Him, our neighbor, and the other selves in the dynamic triad of faith. Hoedemaker puts it nicely when he says that we will thus be able to see *one action* coming down upon us in *all the actions* that come down on us. And then we will be enabled to see God the Creator, Governor, and Redeemer sending one Divine Action, and not three on us.

Some Critique of Niebuhr's Ethics

While Niebuhr's Ethics of Responsibility is a very good instrument for analyzing the moral experience, it is not beyond criticism. I have chosen to focus on the views of a few of his critics in brief terms. They are: Libertus Hoedemaker, James Fowler, James Gustafson, and Thomas R. McFaul. These men focus their criticisms mainly on: 1) Niebuhr's analysis of the fundamental structure of the moral life, and 2) his method of decision-making.

All the above critics argue that Niebuhr conveys a passive impression of human agency by stressing the primacy of divine action so much. This is unacceptable to them. Hoedemaker uses the words "paralyzing effect" for the divine action that Niebuhr emphasizes in order to reinforce his critique. Hoedemaker says that Niebuhr places too much emphasis on the principle of being and this leads to a neglect of the eschatological nature of historical experience.[73]

Fowler argues that the way in which Niebuhr employs the concept of radically monotheistic faith discourages any "initiative-taking strategy" in social ethics, but favors "aggressive suffering."[74] Gustafson argues that Niebuhr removes human autonomy with the formulation of his basic question of ethics, that is, "What is God doing?" He says that by doing this, Niebuhr brings in the propensity for human passivity. Gustafson prefers that the primary question should read: "What is God enabling and requiring me to be and to do?" He believes that if the question is worded thus it would introduce greater human autonomy.

In order to fill the hiatus that he believes Niebuhr has created, Gustafson employs an ethic of virtue as virtue according to him stresses character. It emphasizes the kind of person an individual is and becomes, he says. Gustafson also stresses the symbol of the "imitation of God" in his ethics. With the use of this symbol he wants to give the person in its responses to God a larger role and greater autonomy but at the same time "a less precise perception of the divine will."[75] Gustafson wants to think of man more as a co-actor with God rather than a responder to him. Gustafson also calls Niebuhr's method of moral reflection "intuitive." His objection to Niebuhr in this regard is that the interpretation of God's relationship to the moral agent is too embedded in the personal life of the moral agent. This does not allow enough scope for the "remote" relationship that God has to the events of history. The "intuitive method" also pushes the powers of reason to the periphery in moral response.[76]

McFaul's argument with Niebuhr is that he does not give the moral responder enough guidance in the making of moral decisions. He also has a problem with the way in which Niebuhr wants us to respond to all actions upon us. McFaul says that our judgments on influences upon us will not always be accurate as some influences on us are more godlike than others. Is there a more objective means of judgment, he asks? Or, are we thrown back to our intuitions and moods? This is the crux of his argument with Niebuhr.

The above critiques against Niebuhr's ethics of responsibility all have merit and they should be considered very seriously alongside Niebuhr's thoughts. However, they seem to miss the gist of Niebuhr's ethics, but they will be taken into account in my study of Niebuhr. Niebuhr did not intend his ethics of responsibility to be a practical guide dictating to people how they should act in moral situations. He wanted us to understand how God discloses himself to us.

> One cannot expect from Niebuhr's ethics a set of
> close definitions of universally appropriate
> behavior...community's moral life.[77]

Niebuhr says further that ethics is an "aid to accuracy in action and that ethics is no guarantee that we will always respond accurately in our actions." However, while in a democratic society, for example, ethics will not enable us to reach the goal of equal rights for everyone: "It can help men direct their actions by that goal....It enables men to have some objectification of their moral world, inner and outer, and thus contributes to the effectiveness of their action by clarifying their understanding of it."[78]

Niebuhr's ethics does have some shortcomings but I want to recognize his effectiveness and helpfulness in analyzing the moral experience of the people on whom this book is focused. While Niebuhr certainly does not give practical guidelines for appropriate moral action, he does give us guidelines for moral direction and this is what we need in any crisis situation.

The Christian Story and the Human Story

Another important aspect of Niebuhr's Responsibility Schema is the Meaning of Revelation and in particular the way in which it is related to the Christian story and the Human story. Niebuhr's use of this concept is of importance for this study as it shows that his moral philosophy focuses on the particular as well as on the universal. Up to now our emphasis has been mainly on the universal in order to place God's responsiveness and responsibility toward black South Africans in a broad perspective. However, justice will not be done to Niebuhr's ethics if it is neglected to bring the particular into focus as well.

The Christian story, according to Niebuhr, "was primarily a simple recital of the great events connected with the historical appearance of Jesus Christ and a confession of what happened to the community of disciples."[79] The Christian story gives meaning to salvation, sin, forgiveness, God, and revelation. It is furthermore the story of the life of the church. To Niebuhr, any conversation about revelation in the Christian church is a reference to our history as selves as it is experienced internally.[80]

This internal experience aids our understanding of everything that occurs in our lives with greater depth and a broader perspective. Niebuhr contrasts this internal experience or internal history with external history by saying that the former refers to subjects while the latter refers to objects. In internal history we deal with relations that exist because we are selves who are members of each other.[81] These members have a common past which influences their present existence. Our study receives further illumination for its linkage to revelation when we are reminded that the New Testament evangelists and their successors understood history (internal history) as the genesis of their faith and of their comprehension of the world.

> They did not speak of events as impersonally apprehended, but rather of what had happened to them in their community. They recalled the critical point in their own lifetime when they became aware of themselves in a new way as they came to know the self on whom they were dependent....[82]

Niebuhr makes it clear that revelation is found in events that have occurred in our lives and that occupy our memories.[83] By faith the Christian discerns the Divine Self or God acting in and through these events. Therefore the prophets were able to make the connection between God's revelation and the liberation of his people from slavery in Egypt.[84] The revelation of the universal God still operates "...in all events of all times and communities ...all events have one source and goal."[85]

"Revelation means for us that part of our inner history which illuminates the rest of it and which is itself intelligible." That part of our inner history is Jesus.[86] Through him we are able to understand all other events. It is at this point that Niebuhr's christology comes into play.

Niebuhr says, "Whatever else Revelation means it does mean an event in our history which brings rationality and wholeness into the confused joys and sorrows of personal existence and allows us to understand the Christian Story."[87] Niebuhr says, "Through Jesus Christ we become immigrants into the empire of God which extends all over the world and learn to remember the history of that empire, that is of men in all times and places, as our history."[88] This is an indication of the universalistic character of the Christian story and of the Christian faith.

The Human Story is the story of selves who are part of an external historical process, that is, a process taking place in the socio-political-cultural environment that they interact with. This story relates the experiences of individuals and particular communities in their daily existence. It speaks of pain, sorrows, joy, brokenness, impaired relationships, despair, hope, faith and mistrust, life and death. In these human stories those who experience it sometimes find that the way ahead is blocked. Sometimes a sense of despair and meaninglessness creeps in. This gives rise to the posing of hermeneutical questions, questions concerning the interpretation of the meaning of events, things, and actors, in particular those actions that have a limiting effect on them and that often cause injury to the self.

I want to suggest that central to all these hermeneutical questions posed by members of the Christian community is a search for God--the Divine self who is the ground of all being--the one who can make sense out of that which confuses, limits, and causes pain and bondage.

When the human story with its hermeneutical questions is related to revelation an illumination of its dynamics takes place. "We are enabled to apprehend what we are, what we are suffering and doing and what our potentialities are. What is otherwise arbitrary and dumb fact becomes related, intelligible, and eloquent fact through the revelatory event.[89] Furthermore, says Niebuhr,

"Revelation means the moment in which we are surprised by the knowledge of someone [God] there in the darkness and the void of human life; it means the self-disclosure of light in the darkness" (brackets mine).[90] Revelation is the time we are given a new faith. The God who reveals himself in Jesus, we learn to trust in every facet of our human story.

That faith with which we learn to trust Jesus is a radical monotheistic faith that enables us to trust firmly in God and to respond to everything and every event, every limiting force as if responding to Him--to reword our hermeneutical question with new insight and faith with the words: "What is God doing?" This opens up the possibility for God's peace and understanding, grace, reconciliation, and restoring power to fill the void in our lives. We learn afresh and anew that "God's rule is present in whatever happens...."[91]

The human story is a story in which Christ's process of revelation has begun but not completed [in our lives] (brackets mine).[92] It is a story in which we interpret and respond. It is a story which has its existence in sin but yet within the hope of salvation.[93]

CHAPTER 3

AN ETHICAL-PSYCHOLOGICAL MODEL

When a study is conducted of parents in relation to children it is important to approach such a study from an ethical-psychological perspective. However, ethics and psychology should not be employed on a general level. We must be specific. Therefore the author of this book selected Erikson and Niebuhr to achieve this goal. This chapter focuses on a model which illustrates how these two disciplines could be integrated. It must be pointed out, however, that this is a miniature version of an attempt to show how the merging of ethics and psychology enables us to shed light on intergenerational problems. When dealing with intergenerational relationships a deficiency will occur if we deal with such relationships solely on ethical or psychological terms. There must be an integrated approach in which both are employed.

Scholars are employing models in various situations to make possible the emergence of more reliable insights and disclosures about various phenomena. Models are being used in science, psychology, and theology with great benefit to these disciplines. What is a model? For this explanation I am relying heavily on the book of Ian Ramsey, *Models and Mystery*.[1] While we could formulate a definition of models from more than one perspective the most ordinary description is given by Max Black in his book, *Models and Metaphors*[2]: "In making scale models, our purpose is to produce, in a relatively manipulable or accessible embodiment, selected features of the 'original': We want to see how the new house will look, or to find out how the airplane will fly, or to learn how the chromosome changes occur. We try to bring the remote and the unknown to our level of middle-sized existence."[3] Ramsey says that a model could also be thought of as "a copy picture, something which shares certain important properties with that which it models."

The description of a model as expounded by Black (above) can be aptly applied when it refers, for example, to a model space shuttle or a model of a skyscraper. Ramsey prefers to use the term "picturing model" for a "scale model" as it is a picture of that which is modelled.[4] In the past picturing models have been employed in theology. This was done to understand that which was divine and invisible, e.g., God has been pictured as a judge, a father who sent his son, etc. While these have proved to be helpful, Ramsey feels that "...a picture theology which is too taped and too cut and dried is self-condemned--leaving no place for the mystery and transcendence of God, leaving no place for wonder and worship."[5] Therefore Ramsey suggests "a disclosure model" as an alternative to the concept of a picture model. This is the same as that which Black calls "an analogue model."[6]

> An analogue model is some material object, system, or process designed to reproduce as faithfully as possible in some new medium the structure or web of relationships in an original. Many of our previous comments about scale models also apply to the new case. The analogue model, like the scale model, is a symbolic representation of some real or imaginary original., subject to rules of interpretation for making accurate inferences from the relevant features of the model."[7]

These two models can, however, be differentiated on the basis of their corresponding methods of interpretation. In scale models the emphasis is placed on identity. Here the specific aim is the limitation of the original. In analogue models the focus is on the reproduction of the structure of the model.[8] "An adequate analogue model will manifest a point-by-point correspondence between the relations it embodies and those embodied in the original: every incidence of a relation in the original must be echoed by a corresponding incidence of a correlated relation in the analogue model....Thus the dominating principle of the analogue model is what mathematicians call 'isomorphism.' The analogue model shares with its original not a set of features or an identical proportionality of magnitudes, but more abstractly, the same structure or pattern of relationships."[9]

A model generates a disclosure.[10] Ramsey uses the example of "the edge of a shaft of sunlight coming through a window, along with a mathematical straight line," to illustrate what he means by a disclosure.[11] According to Ramsey, we do not simply observe some form of similarity between the edge of the shaft and the straight line as that from and around both something would "strike us," "break in" upon us. A disclosure is generated by certain features of the phenomena and some features of the model.[12] Thus "the model arises in a moment of insight when the universe discloses itself in the points where the phenomena and the model meet. In this sense there must be at the heart of every model a 'disclosure.' Such a disclosure arises around and embraces both the phenomena and their associated model."[13]

Models therefore aid us in interpreting phenomena. In theology, for example, the "aptness of Messiah and Logos models to the phenomena of Jesus of Nazareth is seen in a disclosure, in a moment of insight, when a Messianic narrative makes some tangential connections with Christian events...."[14]

The model that is employed for the purposes of this study is a model of ethical and psychological dialogue. Erikson's theory is engaged to construct the psychological dimension while Niebuhr's ethics is engaged to construct the ethical dimension of the model. Our ethical-psychological model is constructed with the awareness that the methodology of another psychologist or ethicist could have sufficed. Niebuhr and Erikson were chosen as an example of how, when dealing with problems like those which are discussed in this book, the ethical and psychological impetus can be maintained instead of just one of the two in question.

Human beings are always seeking ways in which they could understand and interpret their existence and experiences in the world that they are living in. In this chapter I shall attempt to show that no single perspective is able to achieve this. This chapter is an attempt to construct an ethical-psychological model based on Niebuhr's Ethics of Responsibility and Erikson's psychosocial theory. While following this methodology I will try to preserve the integrity of both cognitive modes by bearing in mind that Erikson's theory is a study of interpersonal dynamics that focuses on the psyche while Niebuhr's ethics focuses on responsibility based on faith in God.

However, I will guard against giving the impression that Erikson operates completely outside the ambit of theology like his teacher Sigmund Freud. This is not the case. While Erikson is not a theologian he is a religious person and this characteristic permeates his theory without bias or perhaps with a positive bias. In his psycho-historical study of Luther this appears to come to the fore as Erikson stresses the importance of faith for human development. He makes it clear that Luther found his identity through his religious struggles. The implication is that religion is a part of human life which cannot be avoided.

Heije Faber, the distinguished Dutch authority of religion in the light of modern psychoanalytic theories, says:

> Erikson takes religion provisionally as being what it claims to be: An autonomous sphere of life which he of course investigates psychoanalytically. That is to say, he connects it up with other data, but he does this without prejudice, showing neither preference nor resistance.[15]

Psychoanalysts like Freud and Fromm were far removed from religion. Freud, for example, referred to religion as infantile projections. To this Erikson replied: No! It is a component of maturity.

It is of utmost concern to Erikson to draw clear psychological parallels to the evolving insights into theology that become important to Luther during his search for identity. He interprets Luther's growing identity without prejudice in the light of his relationship to God and the Christ who lives within him. Luther's self-awareness was also an awareness of Christ and of the movement of the Holy Spirit within him.[16] Erikson is also not oblivious to the fact that Luther's psychological change and theological renewal were inseparable. He does not seem to deny the fact that growth as a person is also growth in faith.

Faith and the meaning it has for an individual determines how he interprets his moral context and how he responds to the forces that act on him in that particular context. As it is of relevance to the individual's understanding of faith I shall use the concept of ego-identity or identity as it is employed in Erikson's theory. Erikson later discontinued the use of the word ego in favor of self. In doing so he followed Hartman's suggestion that psychoanalysts should rather use the word self when they refer to the object of the "I."

The main pillars of my ethical-psychological model will thus be the concepts of faith which I will refer to as the divine pole, and identity which I shall refer to as the human pole. However, the two poles are not rigidly divorced from each other as I tried to explain above. Overlapping does occur. I shall also look at the correlations of these two concepts with other elements of Niebuhr's ethics and Erikson's theory. The reason for my choice of these concepts of faith and identity is that I believe that an individual's identity (positive or negative) determines how generative or ungenerative that individual will be. Likewise, the nature of a person's faith in God determines the manner in which that person responds to his world and

the people and institutions he interacts with in that world.
I am in agreement with Leland Elhard who says:

> Both a relevant theology and a responsible
> psychology recognize that their perspectives are,
> at least in part, "existential." They must take
> into account that their observations and
> reflections are man's attempts to "make sense" of
> his experiences in the world, to discover his
> center, to organize his wholeness, and to establish
> satisfying relationships to reality in all
> dimensions, including the ultimate.[17]

I shall draw heavily on Elhard's essay to enhance my
understanding of the relationship between psychology and
ethics in this model. In his theory Erikson shows that if a
person's faith can be rekindled it will strengthen the self
and aid him in finding a clear identity. This statement is
reinforced in his portrayal of Martin Luther, the reformer,
as such a person. Through faith he discovered a God who
was not as overbearing as his father. This led him to the
finding of his identity. This enabled him to become
generative not only towards his own family but towards the
universal community.[18]
        "In this context of the experience of faith we observe
with Erikson that the attributes of the ego are akin to the
attributes of Faith."[19]   Elhard draws some correlations
between faith and identity in a dynamic way which further
enhances our understanding of the concept of radical
monotheistic faith (Niebuhr) and identity (Erikson). He
uses the metaphor of "living" to describe this correlation.
He says that "livingness" is pervasive in something that is
alive and being alive depends on relationships.[20] Elhard
describes identity in terms of pervasiveness, relationship,
tension, and change and then relates these concepts to faith.
I shall look at these four concepts individually. It is
interesting to note that when identity and faith are placed
alongside each other then identity illuminates our

understanding about familiar experiences from a different perspective and vice versa.

1. *Pervasiveness*

Tillich speaks about identity as a sense that pervades the conscious and unconscious dimensions of our personal lives.[21] Erikson referred to it as a "way of experiencing accessible to introspection." Niebuhr speaks of faith as trust, loyalty, confidence, and fidelity in God. In this regard God is the object of our loyalty. We trust him because it is He who gives value to the Self. Faith was given to us as a gift through the life and death of Jesus Christ. Therefore we experience this faith in God through Jesus who lives in the believing Christian through his spirit and the fruits of that spirit we also experience and enjoy. Similarly, identity is also experienced in and through the interaction of the individual and his world. By this is not meant that all the forces that act on him and that all the people in his social environment who affect his life mold him into the individual that he becomes.

2. *Relationship*

Elhard, in quoting from Soren Kierkegaard, says that "the Self is a relation which relates to its own self."[22] Putting this in the context of identity Elhard says that "we mean most to ourselves where we mean most to others. Our self-realization is coupled with recognizing ourselves in the context of being recognized by others, whom we recognize."[23]

Niebuhr connects the faith of the believer with his (the believer's) faith in Jesus Christ. This faith can only be accepted and received when there is a relationship between the believer and Jesus Christ. "Faith is...a personal relation to the reality we have learned to call God: It is the reliance of a person on a person."[24] Elhard says further that when we have a Self that is constituted by virtue of the fact that God relates to it then we have faith. This means that the Self has become anchored in the power that is responsible for its existence. This fact also presents a common denominator for faith and identity. Elhard sees faith and identity as relationship concepts. They form a relationship in which faith acts as a resource for identity. "Both point to the self-in-God, where one is fully God's self and fully one's own self at the same time."[25]

3. *Change*

Faith changes and matures all the time as we develop and so does identity. Each experience that we go through changes our identities or strengthens them. In this regard I want to refer to the stages (adult stages) as following the identity stage in adolescence. We change all the time as we solve the crisis of each stage and this leads us toward integrity and self-actualization. According to Niebuhr, Christ's revelation has a continual impact on our life stories. Our idolatries are constantly called into question in the event of Christ and this in turn impels us into a permanent conversion of our faith.[26] Elhard sees faith as the identity that continually discovers itself in God.[27] But faith completes our identity. It is that indispensable dimension that is needed to complete the identity formation process. "Thus we view the end of the permanent revolution of our identity, of our way of life, as living faith."[28]

Identity and generativity are both part of my model. They are also linked together. To place our model in a balanced perspective it is necessary to analyze Erikson's concept of generativity more carefully particularly in the way that it is related to Niebuhr's concept of responsibility.

Responsibility and Generativity

Another point at which the two poles of our model (ethics and psychology) converge is at the level of responsibility and generativity. Eugene Wright says:

> Responsibility is the word that best describes what Erikson means by the ethical sense. He uses responsibility together with, and sometimes even as synonymous with, a number of other words, such as caring, householding, and generativity, but none of these is as comprehensive as the word responsibility.[29]

Wright, an interpreter of Erikson, seems to imply that responsibility is a more encompassing word than generativity. But there is nevertheless an intertwined relationship between them. It is also at this point of convergence where the Self and its relational existence stands out most clearly. Wright says further that responsibility also describes the ethical sense that pervades Erikson's theory. The individual can only receive an ethical sense when there has been a synthesis of childhood morality and the ideological struggle of adolescence. This synthesis makes adult ethics possible. By adult ethics is meant:

> ...a universal sense of values assented to with insight and foresight in anticipation of immediate responsibilities not the least of which is a transmission of these values to the next generation.[30]

The above quotation illustrates how generativity and responsibility merge. The transmission of values is what Erikson would call generativity or the sense of care of the adult generation for the ensuing one. But, it is only an adult who has a sense of responsibility (the firm foundation of the adult's moral structure) who can be generative. This

responsibility in turn is linked to the faith that a particular
Christian adult has in God. Without a radical monotheistic
faith in God (Niebuhr) one cannot respond adequately to
those for whom one has a generative responsibility. Such a
faith enables the person to respond to actions upon him
with trust by acknowledging that these actions, no matter
how painful or demoralizing, come from God. Therefore, I
will respond to them as if I am responding to God.

Underlying responsibility and generativity are
relationships. It is in the context of relationships that true
responsibility and generativity are experienced in a dynamic
way. In Erikson's theory the most important relationship
forming the context for generativity is the parent-child
relationship. In Niebuhr's ethics the most important
relationship that forms the context for responsibility is the
triadic relationship between the self, other selves (also
referred to as social companions before God), and God.
Therefore, at the human pole I shall focus on this
relationship with reference to the childhood of Martin
Luther. Erikson, in his psychoanalysis of Luther's life cycle,
explained the reformer's childhood very vividly. This is a
childhood that evolved in a situation of social conflict in
Germany just like thousands of childhoods are now evolving
in a situation of social conflict in South Africa. Erikson's
analysis of the childhood and adolescent stages of Luther
contribute greatly to the emergence of insights in the
understanding of black youth in South Africa, e.g., the
spiritual and physical environment in which Luther's
parents raised him must have contributed to some or many
of the negative psychological elements that they
interiorized. This in turn must have contributed to the
inner turmoil that young Luther experienced.

> Martin took unto himself the ideological structure
> of his parents' consciences: he incorporated his
> father's suspicious severity, his mother's fear of
> sorcery, and their mutual concern about

> catastrophes to be avoided and high goals to be
> met. Later he rebelled: first against his father,
> to join the monastery; then against the Church to
> found his own Church....We can only surmise to
> what extent this outcome was prepared for in
> childhood by a cumulative rebelliousness and by
> an ever-so-clandestine hate (for our conscience,
> like the medieval god, knows everything and
> registers and counts everything).[31]

All of these contribute great depth to the understanding of
the relationship that exists between black adults and youth
in South Africa. Erikson also deals with the self and God
and the dynamics of the relationship between the two in the
same way that Niebuhr does. This reinforces our model. At
the Divine Pole I shall focus on Niebuhr's concept of the
dynamic triad of faith.

1. *The Human Pole*

    1.1 *Parent-Child Relationships*: The parent-child
relationship is of vital importance to the psychosocial-
spiritual survival of the human species, as it forms the
matrix in which generativity and responsibility take place.
Erikson recognizes this and in his studies on Luther and
Gandhi[32] he places great emphasis on the childhood periods
of these men.
    There are a number of reasons for focusing on
Luther in this part of the book. The main one is probably
that Erikson was interested in theological issues and he
used Luther to talk about them. To cite one example:
Erikson is particularly interested in the inextricable
relationship between faith and trust and how these two
factors are in turn related to the way in which an individual
expresses the self. Furthermore Erikson is conscious of the
fact that theological dynamics, for example faith, have a
great effect on the development of the identity of a person.
He makes the following observation about Luther:

> His basic contribution was a living reformulation
> of faith. This marks him as a theologian of the
> first order; it also indicates his struggle with the
> ontogenetically earliest and most basic problems
> of life. He saw as his life's work a new
> delineation of faith and will, of religion and law:
> for it is clear that organized religiosity, in
> circumstances where the faith in a world order is
> monopolized by religion, is the institution which
> tries to give dogmatic permanence to a
> reaffirmation of that basic trust--and a renewed
> victory over that basic mistrust--with which each
> human being emerges from early infancy. In this
> way organized religion cements the faith which
> will support future generations.[33]

Another reason for turning to Luther in this book is
the fact that Erikson explains Luther's childhood in vivid
psychological and theological terms.   This aids me
particularly in the final chapter to analyze and to
understand the spiritual, theological, and psychological
aspects of the lives of black adults in South Africa.   The
final major point for turning to Luther is the fact that
Erikson and Niebuhr have a similar approach in the way
that they deal with God.   Erikson shows us that Luther
could not have attained his justification per solam fidem
without a deep and harmonious relationship between the
self of Luther and God.[34]   Niebuhr expresses a point which
is similar to the latter by focusing on the relationship
between God and Self in his dynamic triad of faith.
    What these men became in adulthood and the vital
roles they executed in society and the world was largely due
to the effects (positive and negative) their parents had on
them in their childhood years.   Erikson does see an
opportunity to overcome this however.   When Erikson
speaks about identity he speaks about reworking the earlier
stages in terms of a mentor.   In his book, *Young Man
Luther*, Erikson shows in clear terms how the young

Luther's mentor, Dr. Staupitz, aided Luther in the shaping of his identity and enables him to overcome the negative developmental traits that he had interiorized from his father. In so doing, Erikson enables us to see how the earlier stages of the life cycle can be reworked in terms of a mentor. It is helpful to focus more closely on the mentor relationship. Daniel Levinson, an interpreter of Erikson, refers to the mentor relationship as "One of the most complex, and developmentally important, a man can have in early adulthood....The term 'mentor' is generally used in a much narrower sense, to mean teacher, advisor, or sponsor. As we use the term, it means all these things, and more."

According to Levinson[35] the functions of a mentor are as follows: He may execute the role of teacher to reinforce the skills that the young person possesses as well as to encourage his intellectual development. He may also act as a host and guide and familiarize him with the values, customs, etc., of a newly entered occupational or social arena. The mentor is an exemplary role model whom the protege can emulate and "he may provide counsel and moral support in time of stress." The true mentor serves as an analogue in adulthood of the "good enough" parent for the child. But the most crucial developmental function executed by the mentor according to Levinson is to supply the necessary support that the protege needs to realize the Dream.

According to Erikson it is correct to assume that Dr. Staupitz fulfilled the role of the true mentor in Luther's life. He writes that in the winter of 1508 shortly after his ordination Martin was transferred to an Augustinian monastery in Wittenberg. He was then 25 years of age. There he developed an intimate relationship with Dr. Staupitz who was the vicar-general of that province. He became "the fatherly sponsor of Martin's late twenties."[36]

Staupitz soon became aware of Martin's gifts, intellectual abilities, and inner conflicts. But he had great faith in him. He had "the rare ability of making a younger man feel that he is understood." Martin "in turn responded with a complete and tenacious father transference of a positive kind...." When the reformation came Luther continually verbalized the fact that it was Staupitz who "saved him when he was about to drown [ersoffen] in his temptations, but also with having provided him with some specific fundamental insights on which the future wholeness of this new theology was to be based."[37] Erikson says:

> That shift in self-awareness, however, cannot remain confined to professional partnerships such as the observer's with the observed or the doctor's with the patient. It implies a new ethical orientation of adult man's relationship to childhood: to his own childhood, now behind and within him; to his own child before him; and to every man's children around him.[38]

The child receives its sense of trust, faith, autonomy, initiative, industry, identity, and responsibility as well as its sense of mistrust, doubt, guilt, identity diffusion from the parent and other significant adults in its psychosocial environment as it interacts with it. The child who, with the help of ethically caring, generative, and responsible adults, has been helped to work through the crisis of each stage of its life cycle would have gained trust, faith, intimacy, identity, and generativity in a parent-child relationship characterized by mutuality, that is, experiences of affirmation. These aforementioned elements form the strong ethical base for responsibility. Subsequently such an individual will be able to respond to its environment in a responsible and generative manner. Wright drawing from Erikson says:

> Therefore, to consider the childhood of great men and whether or not they develop basic trust is impossible without considering, correspondingly,

the sense of responsibility on the part of the child's parents and their society.[39]

When this thought is applied to the life of a great man like Luther we are able to draw some interesting psycho-ethical conclusions that have far reaching implications for this book. Another reason for focusing on Luther is the fact that he also grew up in a situation of great social conflict. Furthermore his family situation was also one in which the responsibility or irresponsibility as well as the generativity or stagnant parent-child relationships came into play just like in the present South African situation. In the following paragraphs I would like to elaborate on and to try and answer questions like the following, namely: Did Luther's parents have a sense of responsibility in the Niebuhrian sense of the word or not? Were they generative parents or not? Was Luther able to achieve a sense of basic trust in his childhood years that form the foundation for the ensuing stages, e.g., identity, generativity, integrity, and a sense of responsibility? The fact must be emphasized, however, that a direct historical study of Luther will not be made but the focus will be on Erikson's psychoanalytical interpretation of Luther.

A closer look at the life of Martin Luther in the context of his relationship as a child to his parents, from the perspective of the interplay between ethics and psychology, will further illumine our understanding of this ethical-psychological model. Luther's childhood struggles and his search for an identity could also be seen as the interplay and tension between the human pole and the divine pole of our model.

From a very early age onwards, Luther's parents sowed the seeds for a negative identity in the growing boy. Erikson says, "Luther all his life felt like some sort of a criminal, and had to keep on justifying himself even after his revelation of the universal justification through faith had led him to strength, peace, and leadership."[40] His parents, in particular his father, punished him very harshly for little things that he had done wrong as they believed that such little things had to be nipped in the bud before they led to bigger crimes. This caused Luther to suffer from a pervasive sense of guilt all his life. But, says William Meisner, the influential American psychiatrist, "...psychologically speaking, we are well aware that the potential criminality that old Hans had to repress with such rigor was in fact a criminality within himself--a sense of evilness and sinfulness that had to be crushed within, even as it had to be beaten out of his little son."[41]

It is no surprise therefore that the young Luther always suffered from anxiety and a fear of impending judgment. His was certainly a young life in turmoil (psychological and spiritual) which had its matrix in the internalization of the rigid norms and values of his parents. Two things that also contributed to his negative identity are his identification with the harshness and punitiveness of his father which stand in stark contrast to his powerless and timid frame. This is reflected in his attitude towards the Revolt of the Peasants when he said, "No insurrection is ever right no matter what the cause."[42] This could be correlated with his identification with the aggressiveness of his father which he had introjected as a child and had made part of his inner world.

On the other hand he also identified with his mother as a powerless, suffering victim at the hands of his father. His mother, in punishing him harshly for small things, was perhaps cruel because she had to be, but the father because he wanted to be.[43] Meisner says further:

> Thus, the brutalizing and primitively punitive figure of old Hans became the prototype in young Martin's mind of the jealous and vengeful God whose loving care of his children was lost in the clouds of destructive malice, unforgiving judgement, and punitive retribution.[44]

It is clear that Luther's parents, particularly his father, had instilled in him a negative identity. The God in whom Luther searched for peace, love, and a solution for his identity crisis became for Luther, like his father, loveless, judgmental, and a tyrant. Luther's inner struggle was between whether he should comply or resist. This formed the basis of his negative identity. The perpetual tension between complying with his father's wishes and the resistance of the vocational aspirations he had for Luther was always present.

According to Erikson a negative identity is an identity perversely based on all those identifications and roles which, at critical stages of development, had been presented to the individual as most undesirable or dangerous, and yet as most real.[45]

This places the psyche of the individual in a state of imbalance. However, the irony of the situation is that this negative identity instilled in Luther by his father, to a large degree, caused such psychological and spiritual turmoil in the young Luther that it led to the shaping of his own identity. This came about largely, among other things, through the discovery by the young Luther of a religious ideology, a system of beliefs or values to which he could attach his commitment and fidelity. This gave Luther a new, basic trust, a deeper faith, and a new relationship to a generative and responsible God. He then experienced God's love and saving power in a profound way. All of this contributed to the growth of new ethical strength in him and the resolution of his inner struggle and the overcoming of his negative identity. This new generative-responsible relationship was the matrix of his own identity, generativity, and sense of responsibility which molded him into the great reformer that he became.

To look back on Luther's childhood in retrospect the following conclusions could be drawn: Luther's parents may have been caring and responsible to a degree, but his father in particular was a hard and brutal man.

> Young Martin was overwhelmed with a pervasive
> dread and fear of his father, which left him with
> a heavy burden of guilt and feeling of inadequacy
> along with a longing admiration of the father and
> a wishful closeness and acceptance that was to
> remain unsatisfied.[46]

Luther's mother was a strict disciplinarian and practiced excessive moralism but it was well intended. She was not as harsh and cruel toward her son as her husband was. However, Luther loved both of his parents as he believed that they meant well to him. "But Luther observed elsewhere how sweetly his mother sang, at the age of 42 he invited her to his wedding, he named a daughter after her, and when she was on her deathbed he wrote her one of his finest letters of love and consolation that can be found in all literature." Instead of helping Luther to build on the morality level of childhood so that he could gain an ethical sense of adolescence and adulthood, the reverse happened as would happen when parents whose life cycles are in a "cogwheeling" relationship with those of their kids are irresponsible and ungenerative toward them. For example, Luther had to keep on justifying himself even after his experience of justification through faith.[47]

The negative and ungenerative as well as irresponsible aspects of his father's conscience he carried with him in adulthood so that he was unable to act "responsibly and generatively" towards the peasants during their revolt in 1525. He even wrote a pamphlet, "Against the Robbing and Murdering Hordes of Peasants." I want to suggest therefore that Luther had introjected the harsh and brutal impulses of his father as a child and this contributed towards his attitude towards the peasants which had elements of irresponsibility and ungenerativity in it. However, there is another way of looking at Luther's attitude towards the Revolt of the Peasants. Erikson sees Luther as providing the theological ideology for revolt against medieval ideas. The young people of that time hooked themselves onto this ideology as it helped them in the shaping of their identity in a time of social and religious turmoil in Germany.

> His dramatic and defiant stance at Worms in 1521 became the watchword and the battle cry of the Reformation: "Hier stehe ich. Ich kann nicht anders. Gott hilf mir. Amen." In essence he provided an ideology which served to resolve the ambivalence of his own tortured conscience and took hold of the frustrated desires and fears of his contemporaries.[48]

By his actions of putting down the Peasants' Revolt two questions could be asked of Luther, namely: Is he losing his integrity in this situation, and Is he being ungenerative? Luther was really saying yes to change by peaceful means but no to change with violent measures. Therefore he supported the princes and became conservative in a sense. The conclusion that we can draw here is that he was acting generatively. Even in adulthood the residues of his inner struggle, which were partially solved in his adolescence, were still there. In a sense it seems to me that Luther was adolescing all the time, even in adulthood. By this I mean that his father in particular had had such a negative, ungenerative, and irresponsible and overbearing effect on his psyche that he was struggling with remnants of the identity crisis deep into the adulthood stage. Perhaps Meisner has a valid point when he says, "Psychologically speaking, it remains a moot point whether Luther's struggle ever achieved any satisfactory resolution or not... beyond all understanding."[49]

While I am convinced that Luther's discovery of God afresh and anew as well as his justification by faith had a profound effect on the context of his inner struggle and the solution of his identity diffusion, I believe that Meisner's point deserves our serious consideration and reflection. In trying to ascertain whether Luther attained a sense of basic trust in childhood it again becomes necessary to reflect on the sense of responsibility on the part of his parents as well as their society.   While Erikson does not state in the clearest terms that there was absolutely no sense of trust in Luther's earliest childhood years he does allude to the fact that he must have experienced a great struggle with trust during that period of his life cycle. The faith of great men is grounded in a fundamental and basic trust. Where there is faith, trust can be expressed. In talking about Niebuhr's theological and ethical structure and the way he developed it as well as the way he discussed the possibility of faith, Hoedemaker makes the following observation:

> When Christian theology speaks about God and faith it places Jesus Christ in the center, for the community in which its work is carried on cannot think or speak of God and man without remembering that it is to the life and death of Jesus Christ that the miracle of its faith was connected, that this is the place where the possibility of trust in the source of being was given.[50]

In order to be able to trust God one must have a basic trust.   It is the responsibility of the parents and society to give this to the child during the first psychosocial stage of life as Erikson describes it. Also, to be able to trust one's self-judgement and self-commitment, for example, in risk taking the firm underlayer of basic trust must be presented.[51]   A large part of Luther's inner turmoil, according to Erikson stems from the fact that he had a great struggle with the acquiring of basic trust from his parents.

In the light of the foregoing facts one may conclude that Luther's parents were not fully responsible and not very generative towards him. We do not want to deny the fact, however, that there was a measure of responsibility and generativity in his parent's relationship towards him.

But it was not enough to enable Luther to develop psychosocially in a peaceful and normal way. But the crux of the matter is that Luther's experience of a justification and a newfound faith and identity in God through Jesus Christ brought about the responsibility and generativity he needed to become the great theological reformer and generative person that he later became. God in his almighty and divine plan for Luther had taken the place of his parents and it is he who maintained a generative and responsible relationship to his suffering, struggling child all the time.

It is important to take a closer look at the way in which Erikson views the way in which Luther's parents are replaced by God at a crucial point in his life. Erikson placed a great deal of importance on the way in which Luther accomplished this. According to Erikson this replacement was imperative as it formed an intricate part of the solution of Luther's identity crisis. It led to a new sonship in Christ.[52] It enabled Luther to see God in a new light and to place his theology on a firmer scriptural foundation. This theological breakthrough led to his becoming the great theologian and reformer that God called him to be.

Martin Luther had a subconscious hatred for his father. Inwardly he was driven to disobey him. These psychological dynamics he projected onto the pope and in particular on God.[53] Erikson views Luther's displacement of his parents, particularly his father, with God as an exercise in faith. His experience of a justification by faith removed the harsh father (earthly) who always judged him and instilled so much guilt in his heart with a loving, gracious God and generative father.

Furthermore this replacement or shift from parents to God gave Luther the needed capacity to recover basic trust in himself and in his "social companions," to overcome shame and guilt as well as isolation that he experienced in such an intense form. It also had to do with Luther's struggle to come to grips with problems of intimacy. Luther experienced great difficulty in being intimate with his father, Hans, i.e., to relate to him. Consequently he also experienced difficulties in relating to God due to the fact that he projected the latter problem on God. However, Luther discovered intimacy later in working with words, i.e., in shaping his thoughts and sermons.[54] His problems with isolation had to do with the problem of: How can I come into God's presence? He later discovered a way of overcoming this problem through the use of scripture. Thus, he dealt with intimacy and isolation theologically.

Finally, the replacing of the parents with God was viewed by Erikson as the solution of a theological problem based on Luther's reconciliation to God. The great theological problem that Luther experienced was that of mediatorship, i.e., How to relate to God. The resolution of this problem aided him in finding a faith. This problem could be stated in another way, namely that Luther was struggling to gain God's approval and thus the approval of his father.

Erikson says further that there are other factors related to Luther's shifting of his focus from his parents to God, viz: He was enabled to deal with a fundamental generative issue in his life, that is, the movement of Christ within. The experiencing of this generative dynamic provided Luther with the mediator he was searching for between God the father and him, namely Jesus Christ. Erikson believes that Luther was looking at the Christ of the inner space theologically. Thus, through a christological discovery Luther solved his identity crisis.[55] Henceforth he could answer the question, Whom am I?, in the following way: By myself I am nothing but in Christ I am everything. Through the latter point Erikson uses Luther in a powerful way to bring out the God-Self relationship that Niebuhr places so much emphasis on. I shall therefore only focus on triadic relationships as Niebuhr explained it in his Schema of Responsibility.

Generativity and Responsibility also take place in the Dynamic Triad of Faith. Only a responsible person can be generative and only a generative person can be responsible. In the context of this triad the actors in it are empowered by God to become generative and responsible. He is the ground of their being, their center of value, and the source of their generativity and responsibility. When God has made us generative and responsible and when we have accepted these gifts from him in a spirit of humility and repentance then his spirit enables us to respond in love and faith to others.

But this encounter with God can only occur when the Self exists in relation to other selves. Responsibility, as Niebuhr describes it, can only take place in a situation of interrelationships, that is, when all the elements in the triad are related to each other, that is: God-Self-Other Selves. And, individuals respond to each other by responding first with a radical faith to God as a faithful and Infinite Self and the Ground of all Being.[56]

The key to the theory of the self as responsible is Niebuhr's conviction of the social character of all human life. Human selfhood is most or best determined by its relation to other selves. Therefore, the social character of human selfhood is of primary importance in the Responsibility Theory of Niebuhr. This conveys to us the idea that morality evolves primarily in the interrelationship of the self with other selves and not firstly to ends or laws. This implies that it is only possible to achieve selfhood and morality when the self responds to other selves.

In this triad it becomes clear that according to Niebuhr, when we look at responsibility from a theological/ethical perspective it can only occur when the divine pole of the triad (or God who is the object of our faith) is responded to by the human pole (the selves in the triad):

> Stated in theological terms this primary question
> becomes: What is God doing? The ethic of
> responsibility affirms: "God is acting in all
> actions upon you. So respond to all actions upon
> you as to respond to his action."[57]

When responsibility is viewed from the above
perspective we are enabled by God to re-interpret and to
re-examine things with the aid of the symbol of the
Responsible Self and with a new attitude of faith, hope, and
trust in God that runs contrary to symbols and emotions we
have used in the past.[58] This is true responding to God.
Such a way of responding furthermore becomes the point at
which the Divine Pole and the Human Pole of our
ethical-psychological model are reconciled, that is, in human
experience.[59] Furthermore, to view responsibility in the
context of the Triad of Faith is to locate such responsibility
or action directly in the subject, that is, a subject who is
responding to prior action upon him which he has been able
to interpret. Such responsibility also gives us a basis and
a moral guideline for interpreting and responding to things
that we are unable to control. It affirms the divine will in
the existential structure of people who are co-actors with
God in their daily lives.

True responsibility also takes place alone where
there is the possibility for dialogue. Niebuhr's triad is a
good illustration of this point because it conceives of man as
an answerer who is involved in a dialogue with his social
companions and with God. And in this dialogue we
constantly hear man asking God: "What is happening?" In
this triadic context of responsibility the individual realizes
that he is a dependent being. He also develops an
awareness that his existence is dependent on an ultimate
cause which calls him to an ultimate form of responsibility.[60]
When responsibility in the context of the Triad of Faith is
viewed from a universal perspective then the following

thought of Richard Niebuhr adds more depth to H. Richard Niebuhr's concept of Responsibility,
namely:

> If a man responds to the demands of a universal God then the neighbors for whom he is responsible are not only the members of the nation to which he belongs but the members of the total society over which God presides.[61]

Christian responsibility as a radical act in God cannot be confined to the personal world of the self. Responsibility is universal. In Christ there are no limitations and in him responsibility has no limits. Richard Niebuhr says that "all men and all societies, all the realms of being, belong to the neighborhood in which this community of Christians is required to perform its functions for the common welfare."[62] In his article, "The Responsibility of the Church for Society," Richard R. Niebuhr focuses on the responsibility of the church for society. However, for the Christian individual as a member of that church the implication is that he also has the same generative responsibility for society and its institutions.

H. R. Niebuhr says that an act or response of an individual can only be understood when the relations of that act and the context of those relations are understood. By this he means that the society and the time in which the individual makes responses to actions upon him is of great importance, that is, the society and the time in which the interpretations of the action is made. According to Niebuhr all our actions and responses are grounded in a particular society, company of interactions, or some history. Thus, when the act or response and its relations are understood I can then ask myself whether the way in which I react to someone who opposes me is directed by "my locating him in the small society of which I am the center so that he is my enemy or in the larger society of those who serve the same cause--be it the life of knowledge or political life or cultural life--so that he appears as the critic of my ideas or proposals; or do I see him in universal society, so that he appears in all his animosity and all his criticisms as my fellow servant. If I am able to respond to the One creative power then I will be empowered by God to place my social companions in the one universal society that does not have the location of its center in me or other finite causes but in the Transcendent One to whom I am drawn by his gift of a radically monotheistic faith in and through the life and death of Jesus.[63]

McFaul states that "it is with this in mind that the radical monotheist develops his understanding of events and of the special role which they play in the disclosure of the divine within the field of history."[64] The Christian who responds in a radically monotheistic fashion will be able to see things from God's perspective. For man this means being able to view it from the perspective of the universal community.[65]

Eugene Wright, an interpreter of Erikson, says that the responsible adult is one who has gained a sense of identity, intimacy, and generativity.[66] In the light of the above we are able to say that this is true. In Niebuhr's triadic schema the person who exists in a triadic relationship with God receives faith which in our model is analogous with identity. That person also receives intimacy which is analogous with reconciliation to the creator and generativity which is analogous with our trust in God by which we live--a trust which enables us to interpret everything in our lives with faith in a divine context and to respond with care and love to ensuing generations.

Assumptions in the Theory of Responsibility

Four assumptions are basic to the theory of responsibility. The reason for mentioning them here is because they form an integral part of relationships as they occur in the faith triad. These assumptions are:

> i) Response
> ii) Interpretation
> iii) Accountability
> iv) Social Solidarity

All four of the above have been discussed in detail in chapter two. Now I would like to show how they are analogous to certain elements in Erikson's psychosocial theory. I want to suggest that Niebuhr's concept of responsibility is analogous to Erikson's concept of generativity.

Responsibility and Generativity

In the context of Niebuhr's symbolism of responsibility persons respond to actions upon them. This response to God can only be effective if they have a radical faith in God, that is, if they believe that all actions come from God. Generativity is in a sense response. Adults can only respond effectively toward the younger generation if they have faith in them and also if they would like to see themselves living on through them into the ensuing generations. We can put it in another way by saying that adults respond to youth with care because they have faith in them.

Interpretation and Generativity

Jerry Irish says that interpretation represents the subjective side of the question: "What is going on?" By means of his powers of interpretation the responsible self finds meaning in that which he responds to. The generative person acts generatively on the basis of the fact that he has made an interpretation which merits his generativity. He has interpreted and understands the relationship between him and his offspring as a cogwheeling relationship of an older and younger life cycle. He knows via his interpretations that he will live on through that offspring. Interpretation can only take place if the individual has appropriated insight about a situation or actions. Conversely generativity can only take place if the adult has appropriated insight about the life stage and psychosocial situation and context of youth.

Accountability

In the context of Niebuhr's responsibility theory accountability refers to expectations that a self has of reactions to its responses. The generative self also expects reactions to its response of generativity (care). The parent expects the child to appreciate his love and care, and to reciprocate it.

Social Solidarity

This is the final component in responsibility from Niebuhr's point of view. It is related to generativity as follows: Generativity takes place in a continuing community of agents (that is, ensuing generations). All the time the adult is forming and molding the personality of the youth in a continuing process. By the same token social solidarity implies that there is continuity in the community of agents to which the responses of the self are made. These responses occur in a continuing process between the self and God; the self and social companions; and the self and social companions and God.

On the psychological side it may be stated that when the continuity or "cogwheeling" between adult and ensuing generations or youth stops we have a state of self-absorption or preoccupation with the self. This is also referred to as stagnation, the opposite pole of generativity by Erikson. On the theological side where a continuing process with God and social companions stops, despair develops. Despair could be referred to as the opposite of faith. It can also be called sin. This despair can be linked to an indifference to the Self-God relationship which results in a failure to be the new creature in Christ or the new self that is only possible in a continuous relationship of faith with God through Christ. Stagnation, indifference, and sin also affect the identity formation of the self.

It is not possible to have an identity without a relationship to somebody. In the case of the child it is the parent(s). And when we speak in terms of the ultimate identity we know now that it cannot be achieved without God through Jesus Christ. There can be no social solidarity or companionship which allows one to have faith, without relationship. This identity relationship and faith relationship form the strong pillars that give us a sense of self.

The Self as a Connecting Point Between Ethics (Niebuhr) and Psychology (Erikson)

1. *Erikson's Ideas About the Self*

For Erikson the idea of the Self is connected to the concept of identity. "Identity in its vaguest sense suggests, of course, much of what has been called the Self by a variety of workers, be it in the form of a self-concept, a self-system, or in that of fluctuating self-experience described by Schilder, Federn, and others."[67]

Erikson finds it helpful to refer to Hartman's usage of the concept of Self. Hartman gives us an interesting perspective on the Self. He prefers to speak about "self-representation" instead of "object representation."[68] According to Erikson, when we speak of Self in the Hartmanian sense of the word we become aware of the indispensable role played by the ego in this self-representation.[69] The ego is a "central and partially unconscious organizing agency" whose function it is to "deal with a changing self which demands to be synthesized with abandoned and anticipated selves."[70] Throughout the childhood stages in Erikson's theory various images of the self are exhibited. During the identity vs. identity confusion stage in adolescence these self-images are integrated after going through a number of crises in childhood. And, this process evolves into what Erikson refers to as a sense of identity. Erikson also refers to this sense of identity as Self-Identity which "emerges from experiences in which temporarily confused selves are successfully reintegrated in an ensemble of roles which also secure social recognition."[71] In the past Erikson referred to identity as ego identity. For Erikson "ego identity (on the other hand) could be said to be characterized by the actually attained but forever-to-be-revised sense of the reality of the self within social reality."[72] The "selves" which constitute the composite self have counterplayers which are labelled the "others." The "I" which is a conscious entity constantly compares these selves with the "others." That is why Erikson is in agreement with the suggestion made by Hartmann, namely that "ego" which is unconscious should be replaced by the word Self as the object of the "I."[73]

2.1 *H. Richard Niebuhr's Idea of the Self*
2.2 *Points of Congruence Between the Selves of Niebuhr & Erikson*

Niebuhr believes that the self has a relational existence. This point is explained in detail in chapter 2 of this book. Hoedemaker, an interpreter of Niebuhr, says that the self is social and knows itself only in relation to other selves. According to Niebuhr the (one) self executes many roles. But, it is one self that is present in all the roles. On a congruent level with Niebuhr, Erikson also speaks about the many roles of the self that it has to fulfill. But the important fact is that it is during adolescence that these role images are integrated.[74]

Niebuhr elaborates on the above point as follows: "When we say that the power by which we are is God, we may express our interpretation in trust...God means the affirmer of our being, not its denier."[75] The latter point could be formulated in another way, i.e., the Christian self receives its identity in Christ. One of the ways in which this comes about is that this self pledges its fidelity to an ideology which in this case is the Christian religion. Niebuhr says: "Our primordial interpretation of the radical action by which we are is made in faith as trust or distrust."[76] Niebuhr is thus saying that the way we perceive ourselves as individuals with an identity from a Christian perspective is done on the basis of a faith in God. Erikson expresses a thought which is harmonious with Niebuhr's latter statement. He says that in the adolescent stage of the life cycle the young person receives an identity when he pledges his faith and trust to the "affirmers of our beings" which in this case (on the psychological level) are our parents and society. In line with this mode of thought Niebuhr says:

> To respond to the ultimate action in all responses to finite actions means to seek *one* integrity of self amidst all the integrities of scientific, political, economic, educational activities...the *ONE* beyond all the finite systems.[77]

To place the above thought on a congruent level as far as Niebuhr and Erikson are concerned, I would formulate it in the following way: In psychology the affirmation of self comes through a person or persons, e.g., parents, but in theology or in the case of Niebuhr's ethics it goes beyond the person to a transcendent source, to the *ONE* beyond people, human activities, and human systems.[78]

Furthermore, in ethics the question of freedom of the self arises. This freedom can only come about when the self is able "to change its past and future and to achieve or receive a new understanding of its ultimate historical context. If these two modifications are possible, then reinterpretation of present action upon the self must result, and a new kind of reaction, a response that fits into another lifetime and another history, can and will take place."[79]

How does Erikson view this freedom of the Self? I would venture to say that if Erikson viewed the freedom of the self from the perspective of the adult stages of the life cycle he would probably refer to it as generativity. There needs to be a new reinterpretation by the adult of his role and responsibilities towards the youth. The generative adult is one who has been liberated from the "bondage" of the crisis of the stages of the life cycle that precede the generative stage. This new reinterpretation will enable a new response or a new, generative relationship to evolve between adults and youth. Through generativity youth could obtain a new freedom psychologically with the aid of adults who care about them. I would like to refer to this new psychological freedom as liberation from identity confusion and the achievement of a positive identity. Adults who aid the youth to solve the crisis of their identity vs. identity confusion stage are in a sense aiding them in "a reorganization of the past."[80]

The self also affects its social companions (others with whom it interacts in its psychosocial environment) and is affected by them in turn. This thought is stressed by Niebuhr on many occasions. For it he is indebted to George Mead and his understanding of the self as a "socius." This latter thought is discussed in detail in chapter 2 of our book. Erikson refers to these social companions or other selves in Niebuhrian terms as *counterplayers*. This encounter of the self with other selves (counterplayers) takes place in the context of a network or pattern of relations. Niebuhr speaks about this pattern of relationships or relational existence in terms of response and responsibility.[81] Erikson speaks of this encounter in psychosocial terms. Christ alone can bring this about by means of a radical transformation. This is a transcendence and a transformation that goes far beyond the processes of socialization and development of the individual as they are understood in psychological terms. But we should not dismiss psychology and the usefulness of psychological insights for theology so easily. In this regard I must mention the helpfulness and value of Erikson's insights for pastoral care. Erikson does not dismiss the transcendent factor. This factor is supported by the "positive bias" that he gives to faith and God in Luther's struggles for identity and the connection of the inner space with the religious realm. This should be borne in mind by the pastoral theologian.

Homans says further in his article, "Towards a Psychology of Religion,"[83] that "one encounters God as one moves away from or perhaps I should say as one moves 'beyond' the effects of development and socialization as exclusively formative of the self. In such fashion theologians protect theological meaning from being reduced to psychological interpretation."[84]

If one looks at our ethical-psychological model from Reinhold Niebuhr's perspective it becomes evident that he assigns psychology to the realm of "nature" and to the study of psychopathology and adjustment. But he divorces it from the analysis of the dramas of the self and of history. He says that analysis from a psychological angle cannot penetrate the uniqueness of the spirit as it appears in the dramas of history.[85] Niebuhr is too harsh in his criticism of psychology. Erikson has proved that he is not just a psychopathologist and that his theory is helpful in analyzing the dramas of the self and history. Every phase or stage of the life cycle is a critical drama and a crisis which Reinhold Niebuhr seems to overlook. And Erikson has been of great value in sharpening our understanding and insights about these crucial dramas.

I believe that Homans puts the tension between psychology and theology in a much more balanced perspective than Reinhold Niebuhr with his thought that when psychology is applied to the self in order to interpret psychodynamic processes in the psyche of the person it may give us only a partial meaning of the person and its total existence. And it is at this point where theology takes over from psychology. Erikson, I believe, suggests in more ways than one that he is in agreement with this latter point. Time after time he refers to the Holy, the Face, and the numinous in the evolvement of the self but he does not give the impression that the self can be understood without it and the faith factor. While my model has limitations I believe that it could make a valuable contribution to existing models and methods used by pastoral theologians to analyze and understand the moral predicament of Christians, particularly those who are embedded in conflict situations like South Africa.

The Significance of Trust in
Niebuhr and Erikson

Another point at which Erikson's and Niebuhr's thinking converge is at the point of trust. The element of trust, as it occurs in Niebuhr's theology and his responsibility schema, is used synonymously with faith. "Faith [or trust] is the attitude of the self in its existence toward all the existences that surround it, as beings to be relied upon or to be suspected"[86] (brackets mine).

Niebuhr says further that this faith which operates as trust or distrust is found in all interactions with our social companions and it determines the way in which we respond toward them.[87] It also forms the basis of our hermeneutical action of that agency which brings or has brought us into being as selves.[88] We can also respond to that action which is responsible for our existence, namely the power of God, in faith as trust or distrust. It is God, the "one beyond all the many,"[89] "the ultimate action in all responses to finite actions" who gives integrity to the person as a self. To believe the opposite is to dwell in mistrust and lack of faith. It means furthermore that the answers to our hermeneutical questions about our existence will cause us to be unresponsive and irresponsible and to be unable to see God acting in all actions upon us as Niebuhr explains. It is also to misplace our center of value and integrity.

Psychologically this faith that Niebuhr speaks about is synonymous with basic trust or basic mistrust that the infant experiences in the first stage of Erikson's stage theory. This basic trust later evolves into religious faith or into unbelief as the child grows older. Subsequently it determines the kind of self that that child will become. It also determines what kind of ideologies it will adhere to and ultimately whether it will become a responsive and responsible or irresponsible, generative or ungenerative adult and what kind of trust it will develop, e.g., a trust or faith that is monotheistic or henotheistic.

Therefore the relationship with the mother is so crucial. At the human level (human pole of the model) it is as important as our relationship to God (divine pole of the model). Erikson refers to this earliest relationship as a "sense of a hallowed presence" which "contributes to mankind's ritual--making a pervasive element which is best called the numinous."[90] This numinous presence of the mother forms the basis of the sense of "I" which that infant will acquire as it develops and matures.[91]

Loyalty and Fidelity

Another point at which Niebuhr's ethics and Erikson's theory converge is at the point of fidelity and loyalty. As with trust, Niebuhr uses the concept of fidelity with faith and loyalty. He also refers to fidelity as "... devotion to a cause and a disciplining of actions in service to a cause."[92] Faith as fidelity and loyalty pervades Niebuhr's sense of response and responsibility by a self to the One beyond the many. This loyalty as Niebuhr uses it is loyalty to a Center of Value, that is, to that which gives it integrity and self-worth. This loyalty is pledged to a

cause or a god because of the confidence that the self is able
to have in the god who is its center of value and the ground
of its being.

At the psychological pole the propensity for fidelity
is most intense in the adolescent stage as the youth
struggles to establish an identity. They seek for ideologies
that they can pledge their fidelity to and they temporarily
over identify with the "heroes of cliques and crowds" in their
search for an object of fidelity and in an attempt to define
their own identity.[93] This causes the young person to
experience a temporary loss of identity. He experiences
difficulty in extracting himself from this psychological state
of mind by his own power.[94]   This is where another
limitation factor crops up in Erikson's theory as a tool for
pastoral counseling and care of youth. This is also where
Niebuhr's ethics of responsibility is an aid particularly in its
reference to the "One beyond the heroes of cliques and
crowds" who can create order out of chaos and confusion
and extract the youth with their identity confusion from this
personality crisis.

CHAPTER 4

THE STORIES OF FIVE ADULTS

Case Studies

INTERVIEW WITH MR. E.

H1:   If you looked at your life as a story that came in chapters, what would those chapters be?

E1:   I come from a family of four children. We lived in W with our father and mother before we were forced to leave our home under the "Group Areas Act." I had happy childhood years near our church with an old tradition and our church school where I received my basic education. At the age of 12 the area where we lived was declared a "White residential area" in terms of the Group Areas Act and the government forced us to live in a new area for black people. I did not understand things well but it made a vivid impression on my mind. We had to make new friends. When I completed high school the "Group Areas" came once more and declared our new place of residence a "White residential area." Again we were forced to move. Then came the big shock in my life. I became older and could understand things better.
I asked myself: Why should black people be chased out of their homes every time. This made a very vivid impression on my mind against an unjust system where our people were disenfranchised, had no rights, and had to endure a government system that was forced down on them by people whom they were not allowed to elect because they had no voting rights.

During my senior year in high school I committed my life to Christ and went to study theology.

During my student years that unjust system I experienced in my childhood years grew and grew. I tried to look for answers in the Bible and in my own theological reflection and had to look for people who thought the way I did about things. In later years I became a member of the Christian Institute and remained a member until it was banned in 1977. This was a Christian, activist organization. I realized my helplessness more and more as people came to me, people who came in touch with my ministry and theological reflection--people who were also disadvantaged through the Group Areas Act and other discriminatory laws. This forced me to come to one conclusion, namely, that no structures in the world are permanent. If these structures are made by man we as Christians should strive toward the "intervening of righteousness." This became the pattern of my whole ministry, my whole life pattern. I am still in the ministry and I try to be active in the community and to help people through my ministry to see all these things, to analyze these things, and to see where and how we can bring justice into these unjust structures in peoples' relationships.

Two main chapters in my life are as follows. The first one was to be robbed of my roots by the Group Areas Act of the South African government. This was the biggest negative experience in my life. The fact that I found Christ in my life may have compensated for it, compensated for much bitterness. This fact enabled me to work through the injustices in our society with less bitterness and to change that which I could and to alleviate the suffering of others. You know, whenever I go to my birthplace and see that there are other people living there now (white people) and realize that I am not allowed to live there by law; when I go to the second area to which we were forced to go and notice that all those homes have been demolished and that there are just a few lonely trees standing there; when I go to the church where I was baptized, laid down my confession in Jesus Christ, my confession of faith, the place where I lived my happy childhood years and see that old, historic building that was wrenched out of our hands, then my heart fills with sorrow. Then I am filled with a determination to strive toward the day when we could have all that back again because it is really ours. I think this is what we should all strive for in South Africa. In the new South Africa--those who were robbed of their property should get it back again.

The other chapter was when I became a member of the Christian Institute and entered the ministry. The fact that I could further my studies, travel to Europe to get a wider exposure in the world, to see the church in universal context gives one hope and encourages one to fight harder for justice in South Africa.

H2:   How does a parent care for a child in a crisis situation?

E2:   It is a very painful experience to raise your child in a militarized society. Let me give an example. My son is five years old. And there are parents who think that when a child is five years old the environment makes no impression on him. But the events under the "Emergency Situation" in South Africa with police, army, "Caspers" seen everywhere in the streets have had an indelible impression on his mind. My five-year old would run into our house when the police approach because his friends have said to him: You must run away when they come because the police shoot and kill children. When you have to educate and raise your five-year-old in such a militarized environment where you live in fear every moment is very tough.

I have certain convictions that have grown with me over the years. That is, that I will fight for righteousness. This is #1. I would never relinquish this principle. But now you come into a congregation where people are basically conservative because it is easier for people to do nothing, not to land in trouble and to keep quiet. I cannot push aside my values and my divine command, that is, to preach. However, I try not to work with political statements as my point of departure. But I try to win the trust of my congregation first via a good pastorate. But through this I let the Bible speak and allow the Bible message to reflect on the concrete reality in South Africa. Therefore my preaching also has a social-ethical and political dimension. But I also try to use a good and basic exegesis so that I don't just make political statements from the pulpit every Sunday. My point of departure is an interpretation of the Word so that my congregation walks with me, so that when the application of the message is made they understand or begin to understand these applications as they come from a good theological base. This I have seen in the past eight months that I have been in my new congregation since my return from the University of Amsterdam. I have seen the positive effects of the above on my congregation as well as the trust that they have developed in me.

But now I am part of a community as well and the kids have landed in a difficult situation with the school boycotts. One night during the school boycott period about 22 kids were arrested. The charges that the police brought against them were for intimidation, fostering violence, participating in violence, etc. The ages of the kids ranged from 15 to 17 years. That night from 10:00 onwards the phone rang nonstop. Parents were frantic. They wanted help for their detained kids. I called several colleagues immediately. We formed a support committee that night to support the kids who had been detained. We appeared in court three times on behalf of the kids. It was then that the committee won the trust and confidence of the parents more and more as well as that of the kids. When they saw that their minister and his colleagues stood by them in the time of crisis they began to view their ministers and their church in a new light. I was elected as the secretary of this committee.

We raised funds to pay for the lawyers who represented these kids. The community supported us. I had a choral evening at my church as a fund raising effort. This effort brought in a substantial amount of money that went toward legal fees. Now we have decided to establish a more permanent body with its own constitution. It will be a civic body and it will endeavor to represent and support other aspects of community life that need attention too.

H3:   Does the South African apartheid situation limit your parenting functions?

E3:   Every situation that tries to curb human life is an ideology. There are good as well as bad ideologies. But the apartheid ideology is a bad one because it tends to control the total existence of black people in a negative way. It protects the interests of one group, that is, the white group. It prevents me as a parent from being a full human being and parent. This system wants to play god. God alone is in charge of the totality of my existence. That is why the apartheid system must be destroyed. The question is: How are we going to destroy it? I think we must first destroy the economic base that supports it. In this way they won't have capital to build up their great military power which they use to intimidate black kids and their parents. All of this is linked to the economic power of the system and the execution of this power. I think that the present economic crisis, e.g., the crumbling of the stock exchange, etc., are all good signs. It illustrates that the idol is busy crumbling and that the idol is not god.

Apartheid limits one in everything that one does. It prevents one from being a parent because apartheid affects one's ability to be human, e.g., the child loses total respect for the parent. If I as a parent have to tell my child that we cannot walk on a particular beach because of the notices then that "Whites Only" notice breaks down my parental authority. The child who has to look up to that parent sees how powerless that parent is. That child witnesses a policeman removing him and his parents from a beach where they are not allowed to be because they are black. This is one example of how apartheid breaks down parental authority. There are many other examples. Apartheid puts a label of inferiority on me.

H4:   Has your personality changed over the past ten years?

E4:   One can change for the better or for the worse. I
       have become more convinced over the past ten years
       that this system must be destroyed.
       I have become more determined to fight this
       apartheid system. It has become a matter of life and
       death to me. So, I guess my personality has become
       more aggressive towards the evil in our society that
       has to be eradicated. My personality has also
       matured in such a way that it accommodates the
       legacy that I want my kid to have more deeply. I
       want those values that I taught him to be carried on
       into the future to his benefit and the benefit of our
       community.

INTERVIEW WITH MR. D.

H1:   Mr. D, if you looked at your life as a story that came
       in chapters, what would those chapters be?

D1:   I was born in M on October 22, 67 years ago. In the
       "early days" when I was a child life was much better
       than today because in those days blacks and whites
       lived together. That was before the apartheid laws
       and the separation of the races became legal in this
       country. We all enjoyed everything together. We
       went to the same schools. When we are one people
       then the prospects for the future are better. In 1948
       apartheid was born with the coming into power of
       the Nationalist government and the Afrikaners. The
       blacks were pushed to the sideline because the
       Afrikaners wanted to be a "pure race" like the Nazis.
       That's why they brought about laws like the "Group
       Areas Act" that took away land that we owned and
       dumped us in places that we did not want against
       our will with meager compensation. All those

apartheid laws were aimed against our people, to dehumanize and to destroy our dignity and self-worth as people. Even on the church level things became segregated.

H2:   What was the parent/child relationship like in those days?

D2:   When a child did something wrong another parent had the right to punish you or to spank you. And my parents would still thank those parents for doing so. There was respect and discipline. Our parents were so strict, e.g., if they said there were no presents for Christmas we were satisfied. We did not fight with them. Truly discipline and respect at that time was 100%. You could never smoke in front of your parents. But today, kids have no respect for their parents. I see it with my own grandchildren. If you tell them to do
this or that, they won't. We were forced to obey. And religion was #1 in those days. Our parents had family altar and regular family devotions at night which were attended by all the children. At night we gathered around the table and read the Bible together from the eldest to the youngest. The black people were all poor in those days. Therefore they trusted God for everything. You see, my friend, if you are poor you can only trust God. Therefore people valued prayer, good, clean living, and good church attendance in those days. The churches were always full because people's trust and expectations were in the Lord.

I was wild in my young days. Dad wanted me to be a teacher. I did not think it was such an important job. I first went to work at the bank, in a very mundane, unskilled position. Pay was very little.

Then at a garage. I worked there for 40 years as a mechanic. They treated me well. I could educate my kids. Today one is a minister, one is a nurse, one is a teacher, and one is a clerk.

H3:   Does the South African apartheid system limit your parenting abilities?

D3:   Definitely. When the kids were small they would ask: Pa, Why can't we go in there? We were then as now forbidden to enter many places. I as parent had to give an answer. I had to tell them with great sadness that it was due to the color of their skins and apartheid. You know, we went to the Cango Caves one day. At the entrance there were two doors labelled "White" and "Non-White" but when we got inside we all converged in one common chamber. How stupid can you get. Apartheid is ugly. Beaches? The beach at B used to be open to all. But then came apartheid and they closed it to the blacks. Yes, apartheid caused many ugly things. It took away the few privileges that we had. Employment? The whites got the best jobs. We were not allowed to belong to the white trade unions due to apartheid. And we were paid meager, discriminatory wages.

H4:   How does a parent care for a child in a crisis situation?

D4:   Every person in the world has rights. I say to the youth: Fight for your rights. You have rights which God gave to all his people. And if one group limits you and takes your rights I would say to them: Every child must fight for his rights. I would not encourage them to resort to violence because violence hurts both parties and we'll lose much

because we do not have weapons. Because the
government possesses all the weapons I believe we
should first negotiate with them. But if it does not
work we should try other methods. Yes, they have
the guns and all the judges. Their people control
the army and the courts. They have all the power.
Perhaps the stone throwing of the kids is not so
good. I also think the school boycotts are not
properly focused. We are fighting each other and
that is not good.

H5:   How would you like to live on through your kids?

D5:   My first desire is that the religious values I taught
them should be carried out. Then all the rest will be
given to them by God. Then they will live for
themselves and for others. They will believe in their
self-worth and will have inner strength. From such
a base they can serve their fellow man adequately.
This is my desire and this is how I would like to live
on through them. I tried to serve my fellow man. If
we seek God first we'll know how to fight for our
rights. I want the kids to fight for their rights. I
tried to fight for ours.

I stood for elections once for the National People's
Party for colored people in 1972-73. I felt that I
could fight for the rights of our people. I did not do
it for money. I saw the problems and the poverty of
our people on the West coast and elsewhere on the
countryside. The Group Areas Act people "took" our
people's homes. I wanted to help to better the
position of our people. They took my home too
twelve years ago and my brother's and gave us next
to nothing. The government sent many people to
their graves empty handed and with tears in their
eyes. They took away that which was dearest to

them. That for which they had slaved all their lives. For some it was a relief from slum conditions. But most people were robbed. It was sad.

H7:   Has your personality changed over the past ten years?

D7:   Yes. There was always this master-slave relationship between the whites and us. Most people did not accept it. I've come a long way since that time. My mind has matured much and I have outgrown the racist indoctrination of the past. I don't accept their nonsense anymore. Yes, my personality has perhaps become a little more bitter toward those who oppress our people and kill our children. But the prayer of my heart is still that God would help me to love and to forgive. It is hard especially when you hide in your house from the bullets and the machine gun fire.

INTERVIEW WITH MR. J.

H1:   J, if you looked at your life as a story that came in chapters, what would those chapters be?

J1:   I was born in W. I come from a family of 10 kids of whom I am the eldest boy. There are 3 girls and 7 boys. I had to leave school at an early age and had to go and work because my father did not earn much. My eldest sister and I left school early to subsidize family income. I went to work at the age of 15 and left school at the 9th grade. My first job was at a place where they manufactured pianos. I worked there for 20 years. Meanwhile I studied through the mail and obtained my high school diploma.

Shortly afterwards I lost my job at the piano factory due to the fact that I was regarded as an agitator and because my political views were not in harmony with the policies of the factory. It was of course a very unhappy situation and a great crisis in my life. I could not find work anywhere in W, my hometown, because my employers had blackened my record of employment.

I was forced to go to another province where I worked for two years to build up a good work record so that I could get a good reference.
Then I returned to W, my hometown. For the past 5 years I have been back in W. At the present moment I am managing a cabinet-making factory. In my private life I am affiliated with the D.R. Mission Church and deeply involved with the sport of rugby. I am the chairman of a large rugby union in Z. It has about 1900 members. We are in turn affiliated with SARU (the South African Rugby Union). This body stands in opposition to the SARB (South African Rugby Board) which is controlled by whites and white capital. Our body is non-racial. This causes lots of tension in our community and in the black sports (particularly the black rugby world) because the SARB makes it very difficult for us to practice normal sport. They refuse to help us to have the same sporting facilities as the clubs that are affiliated with them and their racist policies.

H2:   What effect did the loss of your job have on you as a person?

J2:   I lost my job due to my political stand which was to be involved with my people and their problems and to fight against that which was wrong in the factory and which worked against my people. The loss of my job influenced me in the following way, viz., it made me more determined to fight the injustices that my people faced.

H3:   Tell me more about these injustices.

J3:   Bad, discriminatory wages was one; bad facilities was another. People with the same qualifications and the same abilities as whites were not given the same opportunities for promotion and the same benefits. And the tragic situation of this factory was that it was managed by Germans and not by Afrikaners. These outsiders came to oppress us further in our own country.

H4:   How does a black parent care for his child in a crisis situation?

J4:   Any crisis situation is a difficult situation for any parent, especially in these critical times that we are living in. We are living in a very trying period. The first thing that a parent has to do is to inform his child in detail about the dynamics, causes, and effects of this situation. Two: the reaction of your child towards that situation is important. It is important for the parent to guide the child carefully through the chaos and confusion of such a situation. I as a parent need to ask myself over and over again: What are the causes of this situation. These causes must be spelt out carefully and clearly to the child without destroying that child's balance and in order to give him a balanced view of life.

We as parents have been somewhat passive in the past. Since the first rebellions starting in the 1970s our kids have taken a different approach towards things and towards politics. As parents we have to approach this situation with a very sober frame of mind because our kids see things differently today. At this stage our kids want a total change in the present political situation. That change that they want is the same change that we as parents want but we fear for the safety and lives of our kids in their quest and struggle for this change. Therefore it is good that our kids are beginning to organize because if we as parents did what they did 30 years ago there would have been more positive changes in this country by now.

H5:   How would you as a parent like to live on through your child?

J5:   I believe that values, moral values, are the basic values in any home--the values of religion, a faith in Christ, the value of family devotion, regular church attendance, to have a stable family life, to become involved in the community. To use the talents that God gave these kids and to use them in the service of his kingdom. These are values that every Christian parent would like to give their kids, hoping that the kids would build on this. If my kids do this I would be happy. In that way I would be living on through them.

H6:   Does the South African apartheid situation limit your parenting abilities?

J6:   I believe so. To be a parent under this apartheid system is a very difficult thing. We live in a black project. So, the environment causes the ideals set by the parent in his own home to be destroyed by the vicious, negative environment. It has a devastatingly negative effect on the child's life. Coupled to this is the fact that we have a weak

educational system, bad school situations. All of this
has a negative effect on the child. I want to go so
far as to say that murder is already committed when
your child walks through the project and sees the
situation that his friends who are less fortunate are
in. In this way the child is systematically broken
down. And the parent has to bring forth a white lily
out of the dark mud of a negative, stagnant, and
chaotic environment. This is no easy task. And the
black parent has an even bigger challenge to bring
up the child with a faith in a God who is "against"
all of this, a faith centered in Christ.

H7:   Has your personality changed over the past ten
        years and how?

J7:   One must be a very blunt person if one did not grow
        bigger and more mature during the events and
        circumstances of the past year in this country. The
        whole situation in South Africa made one either
        more hateful, more loveless, or more determined to
        fight for those which are your rights and those of
        your kids in the land of their birth. I pray to God
        everyday to remove the hatred and resentment and
        to fill my heart with love towards the oppressors.
        But I also pray for grace and strength to fight daily
        against the injustices in this country. Sport is one
        tool that I use to do so. This is the gift and talent
        that God has given me. Yes, my personality has
        changed over the past 10 years. I have grown and
        matured in so many ways.

INTERVIEW WITH MRS. P.

H1:   Mrs. P, if you looked at your life as a story that came in chapters, what would those chapters be?

P1:   Reverend, my life as a child was a very full life, not really a life of poverty. But I grew up with many shortcomings because we lived with people who were really poor and struggled a lot. Therefore we grew up in such a way that my father taught us to share with the poor and to be part of the poor around us. This was how I grew up--learning to live with the poor and to help them where I could.

As a younger child things became more difficult. I left home at the age of 13 to attend school in another town far from my home. The schools in our country town only went as far as grade 4. This was difficult. I lived with a widow who had six other boarders. Those high school years were not so bright. They were tough. I did not study further on completion of high school. Three years after that I got married. This changed my life completely. The first year of marriage was very difficult. There were many hardships and we had to move around a lot, due to the fact that my husband did various kinds of jobs. We started in town A. Our eldest son was born in town B. We lived here for four years where my husband was a bus driver. Due to low wages we left for town C where he worked for his brother who had a business. We lived there for 5 years. Then we moved to town D where my husband worked as director of a Youth camp for boys. We stayed there until the camp was closed down. Then we moved to town E where we lived for seven years. My husband worked here in business and then went to work at sea on the crayfish boats while I taught school as an unqualified teacher for those seven years. From there we moved temporarily to town F. Then one of the influential ministers in our church got my husband a job as janitor/ supervisor of buildings and maintenance at a state institution in town G where we have been for the past six years. I am working here as a receptionist for a medical doctor.

H2:   How does a parent care for a child in a crisis situation?

P2:   Things have changed a lot over the past five years in this country. The kind of relationships that black parents had with their kids five years ago, when kids were still submissive to their parents, is a thing of the past. We find ourselves in a situation now where it is difficult to tell the child to live and carry out that which you expect of him. Today our children are so independent, more independent than every before. They have been forced to become like that. In a sense they are dictating to us as parents. Nowadays they would not hesitate to tell you that you are wrong many times and that the situation in the country is not the way you taught them to believe it was. We did not have this kind of backchatting before. It is very hard for us black parents to accept this new form of behavior that our kids have suddenly resorted to. It is scary and unsettling in many ways. We find ourselves in a very difficult position as we try to raise our kids in the way that we've been accustomed to. There are lots of anxiety, tensions, and conflicts in many black homes as a result of this. Suddenly the peace and harmony that used to exist between parents and kids is not there anymore. Our kids are aggressive and angry. They are restless and impatient with the slow pace of change in the country. The kids are so political and fearless of the police and soldiers. It scares me to death.

H3:   Would you say that the roles of parents and children have become reversed in a sense?

P3:   In the past black parents could tell their kids to do things this way or that way and they would do it willingly without questioning you.   Today it's different. Life has changed completely. We still have some control over our kids but the lives and lifestyles of our kids have changed completely. They do not allow themselves to be influenced by parents anymore the way they did before. Now he lets you understand that things are not the way that parents are thinking. Things are different. My son said to me one day: Mom, it's not like when you were growing up. We are now in a different era. You will have to adapt to this new era. So, it is actually difficult for you as parent to discipline and control your child now. And there are many parents who find themselves in positions where they cannot control the child anymore.

H4:   What does this do to you as a parent?

P4:   I'll put it this way. The events of the past year that hit us so hard created tremendous tension in our home.   The result is that the communication between parent and child is not so good as it used to be. My son was arrested by armed police and locked up during a period of unrest in our town.   They detained him for 48 hours. This was the first time that any member of my family was jailed. It was the first time in my life that I made contact with the law in this way--the first time I entered a police station or court.

H5:   What did this do to you?

P5:   It broke something within me. A feeling came up
        within me as if something had been torn from me.
        I was nervous, afraid, and helpless because I as a
        parent together with the other parents did not know
        what could happen or what to expect.

H6:   So, how does a parent care for a child in a situation
        like this?

P6:   It is difficult to answer. In a situation like this all
        you can do is to tell your child: Be careful, my child,
        and put your trust in God. Try not to do anything
        that can count against you. But many times it is a
        difficult situation. Sometimes it is an innocent child
        who walks into danger. The only thing you can do
        is to entrust your child to God's care.

H7:   So, faith and trust in God play a great role in your
        home in the way you care for your kids?

P7:   Yes. That is all. Every morning and evening I put
        my kids in God's care. I see to it that they attend
        church. That is the only way in which you as parent
        can care for and help your child. That is what I
        believe. I believe that the only reason why my son
        was released from custody was due to prayer.

H8:   Does the South African apartheid situation limit
        your parenting abilities?

P8:   Yes, it does. And it has worsened over the past few
        years due to the fact that this situation has made
        our kids so hard, resentful, and rebellious. They
        now see things that we as parents did not see. They
        now show us things or help us to see things, things

that are not right, and the injustices that exist. As a parent one feels these injustices but you do not have the power to do anything. We are powerless against that which we see and that which is happening. We stand powerless against these forces that oppose us. And in a negative way it affects our parenting. The police with their bad manners, vulgarity, and brutality have no respect for you as parent. They abuse you and dehumanize you in front of your kids. Our kids see this--the powerlessness of their parents in the face of such rudeness. They see our fears and our silence in the face of such rudeness and many times rudeness meted out at gunpoint. Our kids resent this and therefore they take their own kind of action. What do you tell a kid? How do you raise them in the face of such vulgarity and belittlement? It's hard to teach your kids not to hate these thugs but you do it nevertheless. But deep down in your heart you know that they don't buy that, they don't hear you. They may love you as a parent but they want those who ill treat and delegitimatize their parents to be punished.

H9:   Has your personality changed over the past ten years?

P9:   Ten years ago these things did not affect me. I accepted them as a normal part of my life. But the things that have happened these past months have changed our way of looking at things and my whole life. Inside you feel hurt, frustrated, and bitter. You don't see any rationale for the things that have happened and that are going on and why it should happen--just due to stupid political things that oppress us. This government and the group that controls this country are vicious and so immoral.

They have stripped me of my dignity as a parent
and as a human being.

H10:   How would you like to live on through your kids?

P10:   I would like to see the things that my kids are
trying to achieve come true--that they may achieve
it.   I hope that they will achieve it for their
community, for the benefit of the community. I will
give them all my support in these efforts. Parents
cannot stand on the sideline anymore and be
intimidated by fear. Many will be, however. That
is natural. My son who was imprisoned feels that
he wants to study law to help the underdog and to
fight for justice and righteousness for his people.
His detention has no doubt molded his thinking to a
large extent. I feel that he may mean something to
his community one day.

INTERVIEW WITH MR. A.

H1:   Mr. A, if you looked at your life as a story that came
in chapters, what would those chapters be?

A1:   A very important chapter in my life is the fact that
I was given away at a very early age. I was three
months old when I was given away (adopted). The
lady who gave me a home was a pensioner. She was
64 when she took me in. When she died she was 85.
I was already grown. That is the most prominent
part of my whole life. That was my beginning. That
was what anchored me--the fact that I was given
away to a Christian family where I was given the
opportunity to attend school and to finish high
school.   I was given a church. I grew up in the
church and became a minister in the church. That

is important particularly as far as my roots are concerned--in that I know the beginnings. I am thankful to God that I had a foster mother who was sincere and who was Christian. She was a woman who, in spite of her hardships and handicaps, reared me and gave me what my own mother could not give me. That to me is important. I never forget that there was a time when I was nothing, when I had nothing, and when I never could dream that I would rise above my childhood struggles. I thank God for that. I thank "ma" for rearing me and for giving me a chance to life.

I grew up with this large family that "ma" had. She had thirteen kids of her own and some of them had kids of their own. Her husband was deceased. And she had other orphans that she took in. I was just one of the many that she reared. Things were tough. We lived in a wood and iron shack in P. I was baptized in the little church in P. I was confirmed there, became a Sunday School teacher there. This was followed by being made a trustee of that humble little church. I got married there, my kids were baptized there, and one of them was confirmed there. My first job as a pastor was in that church. Yes, my roots run deep in the little town of P.

My very first job in life was as a knitter in a factory. Now I'm doing contracts estimating for an international corporation. I left school at the end of grade 10 due to various problems I experienced. I studied through the mail and obtained my high school diploma in that way. I then tried to become apprenticed as a toolmaker but the "Job Reservation Act" prevented blacks from doing that. Then I got the job that I have at present. This corporation allowed me to do draughtsmanship and I got onto the drawing board. But, I always had this great love for the church and I wanted to do something for my fellow man. When I look back on my life I realize that God has shaped it and is still busy shaping it. "Ma" paved the way for me. She always said to me: It is impossible for me to keep you at school, but the day you start working put away money so that you can pay for your education. I always remember those words. I've always had this great love for the ministry.

Another chapter is my marriage. I am a happily married man. I have six children aged 16, 14, 12, 10, 9, and 6.

H2:   How does a parent care for a child in a crisis situation?

A2:   That is a very deep question you are asking me. My two oldest kids have been involved in the struggle at their high school. But it is a worry. We constantly hear of kids who are beaten up or shot dead by the police. It is really a worrisome situation that we are in at this time. As a black parent one is constantly thinking about one's children, worrying about them. There are sharp differences between my kids and me at this time about events surrounding us. We disagree about many things. The level of reasoning of my kids is completely different to the way we as adults see things, political, economical, etc. The big worry is that if the kids are drifting away from me now already due to the tensions and differences of opinion that the revolutionary situation we're in is causing in my home--if we cannot bridge the gap, then we have reached dangerous ground. The differences are not outside. It is here in our home.

It is causing division in our home. We thought we
were a close family, understanding each other. But,
since the beginning of this crisis I realize that my
kids do not see the things the way I do. We do not
speak the same language. The one said to me: Dad,
it is easy for you to talk. You stand in the pulpit on
Sundays and talk to people. That's easy. But it is
not so easy to DO something about the situation.
You see, she thinks about things from the
perspective of her peers and the pressures that they
put on her. They know her father is a minister.
The kids are even influenced by marxist and
socialist ideas as they search for an end to the
injustices in this land. The kids have become
impatient with the slow pace of change.

We have an entirely new breed of kids today. This
is a new generation. They are on the move. To
answer your question, therefore, I want to talk about
care in the sense of being able to have dialogue with
your kids. I've discovered one thing. This
rebelliousness and unrest that we have has brought
many things to the fore. It has shown that there is
a vast gap between many parents and their kids. I,
for example, may be able to talk to one of my kids
but then not to another. Even the two of them may
be disagreeing over certain issues. I'm trying hard
to save the situation. My child who is in the 9th
grade is leaning more and more towards marxism.
This ideology is busy winning the minds of black
youth. It is happening to all our kids in this
country. And, many of our parents are sitting
around with blinkers on their eyes. They do not
realize what is happening to their kids. In a sense
they have lost control. Children do not take notice
of parents anymore. They say: Our parents were
too stupid to do anything. They feel that they and

their parents are not speaking the same language most of the time. They believe we are out of touch with them. The school boycotts have highlighted this again. Seventy-five percent of parents do not know why their kids are boycotting school. Many cannot see or refuse to see that the whole issue has to do with the future of these youngsters. Perhaps they are afraid to admit that they know what is going on. They are afraid of the lives of their kids as they face the soldiers with their machine guns. I believe there is legitimacy in the school boycotts. There are many things that are wrong with our school system. The kids blame the government for this. This situation of rebellion is not going to change, I'm afraid.

The saddest thing for me is that it is dividing parents and children. Parents and kids never talked about the educational problems that were there all the time, below the surface. Most of our parents just accepted that everything was okey, or perhaps they were just too scared to stir up the hornet's nest. Furthermore, they also just accepted the authority of the school, the government, etc. Our young people have started to question authority and the educational system as well. The problems have reached their pinnacle now. But this matter has also caused tension between parents and children. In many other cases this matter has brought parents and children closer together. My eldest daughter said to me: Going to church is futile. It is not getting us anywhere. It just makes people passive. Church does not reach the real issues. She wants the church to become more militant towards the social issues of the day.

It is also very difficult for me to counsel parents of kids who think like my kids. I become ambivalent in my counseling, e.g., one parent said to me: We do not raise our kids on politics. It is difficult to counsel such a parent. When the kids of some of my parishioners landed in jail for taking part in protests against the government, the parents were angry at their kids for "bringing shame on the family" instead of being angry at the police. It is the task of us as black pastors to interpret the historical and moral roots of the problems in hand to these parents. I also have a fear that my kid will land in jail too for protesting the injustices in this land. So, I obviously want to save her from that ordeal. However, at the same time I have a sense of pride in what she is doing--fighting the good fight. But I am concerned and anxious as her parent. She is still young and does not have enough life experience yet.

H3:   How would you like to live on through your child?

A3:   By giving them an education. Education is a part of my life. If they could get educated and use education to better themselves, to grow and to uplift our people then that in a sense would be my way of living on through them. I would like one of my daughters to become a lawyer so that my fight for justice and righteousness could live on through her. But she wants to become a nurse. I watch the way she plays with her dolls, caring for them, nurturing them. She has some of my helping characteristics. I would like her to do what she wants to do in life.

I would also like my kids to stay in the church. That is number one. I realize what the church has done for me and what it still means to me. It has helped me to maintain my relationship with God. I want my relationship with God and my love for him to live on through them.

H4:   Does the South African apartheid situation limit your parenting abilities?

A4:   To a certain extent, yes. My mother who was white and my father who was black were forced to give me away. In this way the apartheid situation prevented them from being the parents God wanted them to be. Their parenting abilities were cruelly curtailed. The apartheid situation told them that it was a disgrace to be the parent of a black child, particularly in the case of my white biological mother. She was not allowed to have a black baby in the home. So she was forced to give me away at three months of age. Apartheid causes the same drama to be repeated in many homes across the nation daily and in this way limits the parenting abilities of people forcefully. Apartheid brainwashes my kids via their textbooks. It teaches them to be what they are not, that is, less than human. I as a parent have to fight this all the time. In this way the apartheid system makes it difficult for me to carry out my parental responsibilities, e.g., to nurture my children as full human beings with Christian values.

H5:   Has your personality changed over the past ten years?

A5:   Yes, I've changed a lot. The church, my home situation, and the political situation in the country--all these factors have caused my personality to change. Some things are of more value to me now than other things, e.g., my own family. I realized how important they were to me

when I was in jail for protesting against the
government. I think constantly of the many people
who have died this past year at the hands of a
brutal police force and army. This has made me
more caring toward others, a more caring father
towards my kids. I could never realize that I would
have had all these differences and tensions with my
kids. But this situation in my home has
strengthened my sense of responsibility and care for
them. I want them to survive all of this.

Ethical-Psychological Interpretations

Five cases have been selected for analysis with the
aid of our Ethical-Psychological Model which was
constructed in chapter 3. The interpretations will center on
the psychosocial theme of generativity vs. stagnation and
the ethical dynamics of Responsibility and Responsiveness
in the lives of five adults who were interviewed in South
Africa in January, 1986. These summaries will reveal the
fact that the South African socio-political situation has a
limiting effect on black adults in South Africa. The
limitations imposed upon them psychologically and morally
create a crisis situation for parent-youth relationships in
that country. It also curtails the adults' range for ethical
action. These differences are reflected in the difficulties
they experience in being fully generative and fully
responsible and responsive to their youth.

In these summaries we will engage Erik Erikson's
life cycle theory to study the personalities of the adults who
were interviewed as well as Niebuhr's ethics of
responsibility to emphasize the roles of responsibility as
well as irresponsibility in the lives of the same individuals.
Erikson's theory will also be engaged in a dynamic way for
personality analysis, namely that perspective which Capps

refers to as the "thematic approach to the study of human personality."[1]

The thematic approach to personality of which Erikson is the best known representative is very appropriate for the comprehension and interpretation of the dynamics at play in the psyches of black South African adults. Capps states that people respond in characteristic ways when they face particular situations.[2] It is evident that the personalities of black South African adults reflect the dominant themes of generativity vs. stagnation as well as the ethical/moral theme of responsibility vs. irresponsibility in numerous, but not all, cases. The former are psychosocial themes and they reflect the way in which individuals interact with their psychosocial environment.[3] Furthermore, the characteristic ways in which the above adults respond to their environment form the key to the transformation of negative themes like stagnation and irresponsibility or unresponsiveness in the personality.[4]

These themes direct the lives of individuals and in turn affect the lives and personalities of their youth in such a way that they also come under the influence and direction of these themes. It is logical, therefore, that if an adult personality exhibits stagnation and irresponsibility and unresponsiveness the personalities of black youth would reflect the same. In these summaries generativity and responsibility will also be viewed from the perspective of the childhood stages of the personality. Erikson's theory indicates that these earlier stages have an effect, positive or negative, on the way in which the later stages of the personality evolve. Therefore, it is a futile exercise to analyze generativity and stagnation by just focusing on the adult stages. The earlier themes of trust, mistrust, intimacy, initiative, etc. must be taken into account seriously. Children and adults mirror each other. Thus, by analyzing and interpreting their personalities in light of the childhood themes and psychosocial crisis adults are enabled to perceive how their personalities evolved epigenetically.

They are also enabled to view the manner in which they overcame or experienced fixation in the crisis experienced at various stages of the life cycle. By stepping back in a sense adults are able to view the developmental processes of the personality more objectively. Conversely, children and adolescents could be aided by means of our ethical-psychological model to observe what they will become or could become as adults psychologically and ethically. The latter fact becomes even more important if it is taken into consideration that limiting situations like those that prevail in South Africa are allowed to inhibit the psychological and spiritual development of these young people. In this way the evolving generational cycle of stagnation and irresponsibility could be detained.

The following questions were put to the interviewees (they were taken from John Kotre's book, *Outliving the Self*)[5]:

1. If you looked at your life as a story that came in chapters what would those chapters be?
2. How does a parent care for a child in a crisis situation? (The focus was on the present crisis situation in South Africa.)
3. Does the South African apartheid situation limit your parenting abilities?
4. How would you like to live on through your kids?
5. Has your personality changed over the past ten years?

The Story of Ms. P.

Psychological Interpretation

Ms. P had to move around a lot, particularly in the early part of her marriage. This contributed to the fact that she experienced numerous disruptions in the processes of building up relationships, e.g., with neighbors, friends, and the communities into which she moved on different occasions. This was refracted to her relationship with her growing children. The theme of intimacy vs. isolation seems to predominate here. It must have had an impact on her personality as well as those of her kids with an accompanying sense of uprootedness. The theme of trust vs. mistrust must have prevailed as well as they struggled every time to build up relationships. It must have been difficult to gain a sense of intimacy when the dynamics of uprootedness were always there.

In P2, the question of ideology comes into play. Ms. P's kids do not share her ideology anymore. They do not hesitate to tell her that she is wrong, particularly in a political sense. Circumstances in South African society compelled them to adopt that attitude. Thus there is growing tension in the parent-child relationship in the home of Ms. P brought about mainly by societal factors.

In P2, Ms. P declares that her kids "are aggressive and angry." "They are restless and impatient with the slow pace of change in the country." I believe that this portrays the theme of autonomy vs. shame and doubt. Rapidly maturing personalities are detected here as kids are forced to adopt adult roles and to face "adult issues" in their hostile and segregated world. This should not be viewed as negative. Developmentally it could be positive as these kids experience a rapidly evolving sense of "adult autonomy" being reinforced.

In P3, one gets the sense that the roles of parents and kids have become reversed to a certain extent in the P-household. Here we are dealing with *regression* or a kind of "forced-regression" to a certain degree. Ms. P's kids are forcing her to regress and to rework her earlier psychosocial themes so that she could adapt to new, rapidly evolving themes in her children. At the same time this is helping her to shape a new form of generativity and responsiveness to her kids. The accompanying psychological tensions are crucial and acute.

Furthermore, the impression is gained that an acceleration of the psychosocial stages of the children is also taking place as they are forced into the adult stages prematurely.

In P4 it is detected that Ms. P and parents like her are forced into a situation of *self-absorption* by her children and by the socio-political circumstances in the country. She is compelled to turn inward to examine the roots of the parent-child conflict that she is experiencing. It is painful for her to face up to the discovery of certain psychological truths, e.g., a sense of stagnation due to the crisis of parenting in the current situation. This causes confusion. Ms. P thus regresses to the earlier theme of identity vs. identity confusion. This also forces her forward to dwell on the theme of "integrity vs. despair" as she poses the following questions to herself: What kind of a parent am I? Am I failing my kids? Am I caring for them adequately in this crisis situation? Am I losing my integrity as a parent? This situation that prevails has a further detrimental effect on the intimacy between Ms. P and her children. Once again the theme of "intimacy vs. isolation" comes into play here as she and her kids become more isolated from each other.

The jailing of Ms. P's son was an enforced form of isolation and on the psychological level it reinforced the already prevailing state of isolation between parent and children (theme of intimacy vs. isolation).

In P5, hear Ms. P saying, "I was nervous, afraid, and helpless" after the detention of her son by the police. She did not know how to care for her child at that point, how to be generative towards him in a crisis situation of that nature. Society thus forced her into a stagnant situation. In a sense a degree or self-absorption prevailed here. Ms. P was so helpless. The only option that she was left with was to indulge in self-absorption, to turn inward, and to nurture her own fears, anxieties, nervousness, and helplessness against the mighty military government machine.

Ms. P's parenting abilities were severely curtailed by the forces that control every facet of South African society. When her child was detained she became helpless as a parent. There was nothing she could do. She was at the mercy of the police. They would not disclose where her son was being detained, no attorney was allowed to communicate with him and there was no way of protecting him from physical injury at the hands of his interrogators. The theme of "integrity vs. despair" crops up here once more.

In P9, Ms. P says, "This government...has stripped me of my dignity as a parent and as a human being." The theme of stagnation as opposed to generativity is suggested here. In P10, Ms. P expresses and pledges her support for the stand that her children are taking. She hopes that they will achieve their goals. But one senses that while she adopts this stance that the ultimate power of generativity is passed onto the children, e.g., her son "who wants to study law to help the underdog and to fight for justice and righteousness for his people." This point suggests that she as a parent could be experiencing a frustration at her own helplessness to be generative.

Ethical Interpretation

When we view Ms. P's story in light of Niebuhr's dynamic triad of faith it becomes evident that a disruption has occurred in the triad particularly between the points of the triad that are referred to as SELF-OTHER SELVES. In this case the self is Ms. P and the other selves are her children. A degree of unresponsiveness has developed between Ms. P and her kids as she struggles with the problem of how to relate or to be responsible to them in a situation of conflict and uncertainty. She says, "In a sense they are dictating to us as parents." She is thus suggesting that it is difficult to be responsive to them when they, in a sense, make it difficult for the parents to be responsible toward them. Ms. P's function of responsibility towards the children is in a state of jeopardy.

Ms. P as a parent experiences difficulty in responding to these "new children" who have been forced to undergo rapid changes developmentally by societal circumstances. The relational parent-child existence, in the triadic context, has become disrupted. Ms. P says, "It is scary and unsettling in many ways." This suggests tension in the triad.

Ms. P's unresponsiveness and irresponsibility is inevitable. This is indicative of what parents are experiencing when faced by limiting situations and moments of acute crisis particularly in society. Ms. P's disharmonious relationships and conflict situation with her kids suggest that she could be asking herself the question as Niebuhr puts it in his book *The Responsible Self*[6], "What is going on?" Subsequently she wants to know, "How am I to respond?" She does not know how to respond in the face of deliberate limitations. She says in P5: "I . . . did not know what could happen or what to expect." In her situation all sense of value and generative, responsible parenthood is forced to the periphery of her parental ambit. Her only alternative as a God-fearing, Christian parent is to respond to God who is beyond and above the South African government and police. He is the sovereign God and in Niebuhr's words "the Center of Value."

Ms. P wants to care for her children in this crisis situation. Her caring could be characterized by trust, that is, a trust in God. She says (P6), "In a situation like this all that you can do is to tell your child: Be careful, my child, and put your trust in God."

When the responsibility theory is used as an instrument of analysis it is imperative to identify four distinct elements that are inherent in this theory. They are:

response, interpretation, accountability, and social solidarity. These elements have been explained in chapter 2 of this book. They are all interrelated. Each one constitutes a facet of a composite action of an individual or group. Just like Erikson's stages are functions of each other, these elements operate together to form one composite pattern of response. We shall now focus on the manner in which they operate in Ms. P's life story.

1. *Response*: Niebuhr says that our actions are responses to actions upon us. Ms. P's responses to my questions suggest that she is responding to a number of things. To name a few, she seems to be responding to her own fear of the police and soldiers who might shoot or imprison her children. She may also be responding to her own frustration and helplessness in the face of a difficult situation, and finally she may be responding to her own confusion as to how to care for her children in a revolutionary situation. By asking herself the question, "What is going on?" subconsciously, she becomes more aware of the social nature of her predicament. She is a relational person who interacts with others, that is, her neighbors, friends, colleagues at work, her minister, local community groups, etc. All of these present her with conflicting models because not all of them are sympathetic to the "struggle" of the children, a struggle which is connected to their boycotting of school and the "disruption" of life in the community. Furthermore, these individuals and groups (or some of them) are forces in her social environment that impose limits on her. These limits affect her responses.

2. *Interpretation*: Interpretation focuses on the subjective angle of Niebuhr's response question, "What is happening?" If Ms. P can make a balanced interpretation of the dynamics at play in her current disharmonious relation with her children she may be able to resort to

positive response and self-action. It appears as if this is not
fully the case. If she could be assisted by a pastoral care
giver to focus on herself as well as her children as
Responsible Selves who respond to actions upon themselves
in their own individual ways her interpretation could lead
to a new meaning of the psychosocial and moral dynamics
at play between her and her children. And if she could be
aided to see that her children have the added burden of
having to respond in the social context of peers who may be
radical she may become more responsible as she finds new
meaning in a parent-children situation which is responding
to the question, "What is happening to *us*?" instead of
"What is happening to me?"

   3. *Accountability*: When accountability refers to
part of the response pattern of an acting agent, "it
anticipates objections, confirmations, and corrections." Ms.
P is afraid to assume an attitude of accountability in her
responsiveness as the cost may be too hard to bear. In P5
she brings out something about the cost of being
accountable in that situation when she says: "I was nervous
and helpless...did not know what could happen or what to
expect." In a sense she was paralyzed emotionally and
psychologically and was unable to respond. In P6 she
admonishes her children, "Try not to do anything that can
count against you." She is projecting her own unwillingness
to accept consequences of responses she might execute.
These consequences could take the form of hostile reactions
from neighbors, friends, or others in the community who
might have conservative views.

   4. *Social Solidarity*: Ms. P would only be able to act
responsibly if she interprets the actions of her children as
taking place in a context. In other words, she should not
view them as being only rebellious, disrespectful towards
her, or disobedient. She should view their actions as taking
place in a social context, as being part of a whole. Then

alone will she be able to see a connectedness between the actions of adolescence, response to oppression, injustice, and to an immoral society, etc. She will also notice that the action of these children form part of a "continuous discourse or interaction among beings forming a continuing society,"[7] namely rebellious and dissenting youth of previous generations in South Africa. When she comprehends this context of social solidarity she will be empowered within to act responsibly.

The Story of Mr. A.

Psychological Interpretation

The psychosocial theme of "trust vs. mistrust" presents itself for analysis in A1, when A says, "...I was given away at a very early age." The young A must have experienced rejection and isolation. These dynamics must have been transferred to his adult life. He was isolated as a child from the trusting and caring maternal matrix. Erikson refers to this matrix as the numinous or that sense of the holy represented by the mother to her infant. The idea of the prodigal son comes to mind here. A was "lost" to his mother by an enforced losing. But this lostness led to his being found in an intimate, caring way by God, the Father, through an old lady who "was 64 when she took me in." The theme of "intimacy vs. isolation" presents itself at this point in his story. The old lady who took him in gave him a feeling of intimacy and trust which his own mother withheld from him. Through this old lady's caring love, A "was found" by God. The latter point suggests that he then discovered and experienced the ultimate form of intimacy. This led to a rekindling of trust, a new discovery of the numinous which was withdrawn in childhood and in God he discovered a divine intimacy through the ministry. He also recovered the numinous partially through "ma," the old lady who became his new mother.

The generative relationship that he lost with the departure of his biological mother was partially recovered through his relationship with "ma." "She was a woman who, in spite of her hardships and handicaps, reared me and gave me what my own mother could not give me" (A1). "I was just one of the many she reared" (A1). This latter statement suggests that "ma" was practicing a form of "universal generativity." In spite of the old woman's hardships she reared A, her own kids, and a number of orphans. The name of Mahatma Gandhi and Mother Teresa come to mind in this regard.

The theme of "industry vs. inferiority" crops up in A1, par. 3. A says that the "job reservation laws" which prohibited blacks from doing jobs which were reserved for whites prevented him from becoming a toolmaker. Erikson reminds us that each stage is a function of the other. It stands to reason therefore that this theme must have had a negative effect on A's sense of generativity in adulthood. It becomes evident that he did overcome it later. He says further: "...I wanted to do something for my fellow man." The theme of "generativity vs. stagnation" prevails here. It is a refraction of "ma's" generativity into his life--what she did for him and for other children. A also was able to develop the virtue of love through the dominant theme of "intimacy vs. isolation" in his life at that time. His sense of selfhood must have evolved to a strong degree for him to be able to achieve the proper ratio of intimacy and isolation to overcome the accompanying psychosocial crisis of that stage.

It becomes evident that there is an element of stagnation in A's struggle to give his kids a positive identity with values that they could emulate in his life. "There are sharp differences between my kids and me at this time about events surrounding us. We disagree about many things....The big worry is that the kids are drifting away from me due to tensions and differences of opinion.... It is causing division in our home" (A3). The latter is having a stifling effect on the process of generativity in A's life as a parent. There is conflict in the role that A is executing as minister and the roles of his children as children of a clergyman. This role as minister comes into sharp conflict with the ideology of Marxism that is gaining control of the minds of A's children plus the pressure that their peers are exerting on them. The children identify more readily with Marxism and with the revolutionary ideas of their peers than with the Christian ideology and role of preacher of their father. The theme of "identity vs. identity confusion" also dominates this conflict situation.

In A4 there is a confrontation with the theme of "generativity vs. stagnation." The way in which the South African system placed limitations on A's biological parents, that is, a black father and a white mother, and caused them to become embedded in a stagnant situation is further revealed in A4. A says that his parents were forced to give him away. This action was dictated to them by the apartheid laws of the land. "Their parenting abilities were cruelly curtailed" (stagnation). "The apartheid situation told them that it was a disgrace to be the parent of a black child." This stagnation left an indelible impression on A's mind right into adulthood. He acknowledges that apartheid limits his parenting
abilities and threatens his generative inclinations. Therefore "I as a parent have to fight this all the time." He is determined however to fight this cycle of stagnation which is a legacy from his parents and previous adult generations.

Ethical Interpretation

When Mr. A, his children, and God are viewed in the context of Niebuhr's dynamic triad of faith one gains the vivid impression that there is disharmony or disruption in the relational existence of the agents at the three points of the triad. At one point of the triad A's children are located. There is tension in the pattern of response toward God and toward their parents. This is precipitated by the influence of Marxism and peer pressure on their personalities as they struggle with the psychological dynamics at play in their psyches. They have reached a point in their lives where they are engaged in a struggle of faith, that is, how to view a God whom they do not perceive as being generative and responsive to their cause. This places a severe strain on their father's responsiveness and pattern of response toward them. The result is disruption in the triad. We shall now focus on the father's predicament from an ethical point of view by analyzing his pattern of response in light of the four distinct elements that are inherent in Niebuhr's theory of responsibility.

1. *Response*: A is grappling with the problem as to what would be the most appropriate way to respond to his children in a crisis situation. It is a very real dilemma for him. In A2 he says: "My two kids have been involved in the struggle at their high school. But it is a worry." "There are sharp differences between my kids and me at this time...." By differences he means that his and their ways of responding to a critical and dangerous situation are different. That which he regards as appropriate response is not accepted in the same way by them. In his home there is tension in the relationships of the different members of his family. They do not respond positively to each other anymore. "The differences are not outside. It is here in our home. It is causing division in our home" (A2). The "center of value" in the home is also shifting. Traditionally A's family's center of value was intricately interwoven with a radical monotheistic faith. But this connection has now become disrupted. There is a real danger that his children are being drawn towards henotheism, that is, taking one god (marxism) among the many in a pluralistic society and interpreting it as the only relevant one.

This affects A's responsiveness and responsibility towards his children. He has begun to act towards them in an irresponsible fashion not knowing how to respond to an ideology that is threatening the "center of value," a belief in the God of the Bible in his home. "Children are not taking notice of parents anymore....My child who is in the 9th grade is leaning more and more towards marxism" (A2). Apartheid also limits his ability to be responsive towards his children. "Apartheid brainwashes my kids via their textbooks. It teaches them to be what they are not, that is, less than human. I as a parent have to fight this all the time" (A4).

     2. *Interpretation*: When A asks the question, "What is going on?" he has difficulty in interpreting the stagnant dynamics, psychological and moral, at play between him and his children. He speaks about a new breed of kids, the vast gap between parents and kids, marxism winning the minds of black youth, etc. All these factors are included in the realm of his question. In A2 he reiterates that many parents do not realize what is happening to their kids. He includes himself among these parents. What A is really saying is that many parents including himself do not know how to interpret the psychological dynamics that are motivating their youth to respond the way they do. There may be a vague comprehension but it is not adequate to erase the irresponsibility and unresponsiveness that he and many parents are executing toward foreign forces in the lives of their youth. "The saddest thing for me is that it is dividing parents and children. Most of our parents just accepted that everything was okay...too scared to stir up a hornets nest....My eldest daughter said to me that going to church was futile" (A2). The above illustrates the obstacles in the way of interpretation in the interest of responsibility and responsiveness that A and other parents like him are encountering in the present crisis situation in South Africa.

3. *Accountability*:   While Mr. A could not be classified as being unaccountable it is evident that his accountability is embedded in a problematic context. He anticipates and does receive more objections from his children than affirmations. This brings an element of stagnation into his responsiveness towards them (A2). "They believe we are out of touch with them" (A2). Mr. A also experiences difficulty in being accountable towards the parent of other rebellious children whom he has to confront in his role as pastor and counselor. Most of them are just as confused, anxious, and afraid. Even they do not know "What is going on." Most of them are too afraid even to ask that question as it brings out the pain of their irresponsibility and unresponsiveness.

4. *Social Solidarity*:   A's children appear to be subconsciously aware of their position of social solidarity with dissenting and rebellious youth of previous generations as well as those who will come after them even if it is vague in their minds. This is brought about by conscientization in school and other revolutionary groups in the community. A has difficulty with this facet of responsibility, namely, social solidarity. While he tends to be sympathetic towards the struggle of his children and the black youth of South Africa, he is not experiencing a "continuous discourse or interaction among beings forming a continuous society."[8] He feels out of step and a degree of isolation from other parents in his community when he lends his support to the youth. There is prevalent a feeling of disconnectedness in his mind in his relationship with other adults which retards the process of social solidarity. This contributes to conflict in his mind as to the way in which he should respond to the rebelling young people and to the stagnant forces in his country. There cannot be full responsibility and responsiveness on the part of A and other adults in his deprived community

if any one facet of the composite action of responsibility is malfunctioning. The malfunctioning part or element of responsibility in this case is social solidarity.

The Story of Mr. J.

Psychological Interpretation

Developmentally and psychologically it seems that Mr. J experienced an acceleration of the stages of his life cycle due to the pressures of financial and economic factors in his childhood home. This could have had an inhibiting effect on the working through of the "identity vs. identity confusion" theme in his life. He was forced to be an adult in a sense at age 15 and had to assume the adult role of breadwinner which is a heavy burden for a young boy to bear. He was forced to use his sense of
industry in a serious way. One wonders whether he was fully equipped to do so. As a provider he had to "win recognition [in an adult world] by producing things"[9] (brackets mine).

This enforced role of early provider must have placed a strain on the young J particularly in grappling with the problems of identity. Thus the theme of "identity vs. identity confusion" must have been experienced in an acute form by him. It is interesting to note that while there was "psychological disruption" in his life, e.g., acceleration of adult stages in his adolescence which created disharmony developmentally, he went to work at a place where he had to create harmony, that is, by building pianos that would enrich a world that had impoverished him developmentally.

The theme of "intimacy vs. isolation" comes into play when he loses his job (J1) at the piano factory. The job gave him a degree of intimacy which he gained from his interaction with the workers for whose rights he fought. The job loss brought about psychological and physical isolation from colleagues and from a familiar physical environment. The job also contributed partially to the growth of his identity which was in a state of partial confusion at that time. Conflict erupts in a place where he is supposed to create musical harmony. He is branded as an agitator (J1) and his whole life becomes disrupted as a result of this. His political views are not in harmony with the management from their perspective. The theme of "intimacy vs. isolation" is further reinforced when he is forced out of his job. He experiences despair caused by limiting forces which also filter into his workplace from the larger stagnant apartheid society on the outside. "I could not find work anywhere" (J1).

Theme of "integrity vs. despair" suggested here by this experience. "I was forced to go and work in another province..." ("intimacy vs. isolation"). He was isolated from significant others, family, and friends by force.

The theme of "intimacy vs. isolation" continues to dominate his life for a long period. When he returns to his hometown from which he was isolated after an absence of five years he is able to achieve a proper ratio developmentally between the two poles of the latter stage. He becomes active in his church and finds a new and deeper form of intimacy with fellow Christians and with God. This is the highest level of harmony that he discovers after the disruption of the "harmony" in the piano factory and in his life five years ago.

His intimacy is further reinforced in a dynamic way when he becomes the chairman of a very powerful sporting body in his home town. This also raises his selfesteem and he gains a large degree of affirmation and respect, which strengthens his ego in a healthy way. But then the theme of disharmony or "isolation" creeps into his life again. The policies of his non-racial sporting body bring him into conflict with the segregated white sporting body in his country that has the monopoly as far as that particular sport is concerned. This time the theme of "intimacy vs.

isolation" takes on a more universal character. This conflict
later led to the fact that the World Federation responsible
for the management of this sport on an international level
forced South Africa out of world and international
competition. This brought about a universal form of
isolation for the white sporting body. It is interesting to
note that this theme took root in the life of the young boy J,
grew into powerful proportions in a consistent fashion, until
it finally gained a universal perspective.

Now we shall focus on the more personal parent-
child dynamics in J's life. J is sympathetic towards the
political and social struggles that his children are engaged
in (J4) but it becomes clear that his generativity function as
a parent is curtailed by the South African situation. "We as
parents have been passive in the past" (J4). Indication of
theme of "generativity vs. stagnation" with stagnation being
the stronger of the two senses of this stage at that point in
his life. He says: "That change that they [the children]
want is the same change that we as parents want but we
fear for the safety and lives of our kids in their quest and
struggle for this change." With these words J indicates a
sentiment expressed by thousands of black South African
parents like him, namely that they have obstacles in the
way that create psychological difficulties for generativity.
With the following sentence, "Therefore it is good...if we as
parents did what they did 30 years ago..." he reinforces the
negative effects of this stagnation as well as the way in
which the previous generation of adults was embedded in it.

The theme of "generativity vs. stagnation" plays a
dominant role in J's life. In J6 he expresses this feeling of
stagnation in a very vivid way when he says: "To be a
parent under this apartheid system is a very difficult
thing...it has a very devastating, negative effect on the
child's life." The bad educational system for blacks further
stagnates the role of the parent. J seems to imply that
what the parent builds up in the home the educational
system subjugates in a stagnant manner because the child

is indoctrinated negatively.   "In this way the child is systematically broken down.   And the parent has to bring forth a white lily out of the dark mud of a negative, stagnant, and chaotic environment.   This is no easy task" (J6).

Ethical Interpretation

With the aid of the four elements of responsibility as expounded by Niebuhr we shall now attempt to give an ethical interpretation of Mr. J's life story from the above perspective.

1. *Response*: Mr. J experiences tension in the triad particularly with the other selves or social companions. More specifically these other selves are the management of the piano factory where he was employed. He is forced to respond to what he believes is an exploitative situation in the work place. J would view his actions as an agent as responsible but the management interprets it as irresponsible behavior. My guess is that J could have experienced some ambivalence as far as his responses (above) were concerned, e.g., "I believe I did the right thing to fight injustice." On the other hand, he might have wondered whether he was responsible in the actions that robbed his family of their daily bread and perhaps he did not even get full support from his colleagues.

When he returns to his home town after an absence of five years he again experiences tension and disruption in the triad with the other selves with whom he has to interact. In this case the other selves were the officials of the white sporting body who wanted to control his sporting body with a racist ideology. He responds by opposing them. One gets the impression that his is responding in a responsible fashion towards his children in the current crisis situation. This is commendable. However, when the question is put to him in J3, his response in J4 indicates that parents before him (previous generation) acted irresponsibly toward the plight of their children and that he is guilty of that too.

In J6 he declares that it is difficult to be responsible as a parent under the apartheid system as that system breaks down the responsibility and responsiveness of the black parent with it's stagnant influences.   He is particularly perturbed by the negative social environment, e.g., "the project in which he lives" was created by the apartheid system.   This environment curtails the responsibility of the parent.   Furthermore, the school system which is supposed to reinforce the responsiveness and responsibility of the parent counteracts it because it has the seeds of stagnation and irresponsibility in it.

J reiterates that it is a big challenge for parents to bring up their children with a radical monotheistic faith in God who is supposed to be on the side of the oppressed but who seems to the child to support the "enemy." In other words he is suggesting that it is tough for a parent to respond to God in such a way that it makes sense to the child. He would like his child to see his response to God and his subsequent actions towards limiting forces as relevant. But there is always the danger that the child's interpretation will lead to the conclusion that his parents and God are irresponsible and unresponsive.

2. *Interpretation*: J interpreted his response at the piano factory as responsible. He believed that he was opposing an irresponsible and unresponsive attitude(s) on the part of the management (J2). It appears as if J were trying to make a balanced interpretation concerning the critical events in his country (J4). But he also mentions the fear of the parents as they try to face up to the truth of the situation (J4). This fear may cause parents to repress or ignore interpretation thereof.

3. *Accountability*: On this level one must agree that J does display a great degree of accountability. He must have been aware of the risks that he was taking in opposing the management at the piano factory. He must have realized that he risked losing his job. Therefore he must have anticipated their actions even if only to a minute degree. This element of responsibility is thus a strong factor in J's responsiveness and responsibility. However, when it is integrated with the other three elements of our instrument of analysis in the light of responsibility we encounter problems. The other three elements affect his accountability in a negative fashion thereby rendering his composite responsible actions irresponsible to a large degree.

4. *Social Solidarity*: Mr. J is aware of the social context of the problems that his children are encountering and he feels a strong sense of connectedness with them. However it is when his own actions of responsiveness and responsibility are questioned in a context of social solidarity that he experiences problems. He declares that the parents have been passive in the past (J4). This broke down the social solidarity between the parents who in turn could not express social solidarity with the rebelling children. This led to suspicion, mistrust, disloyalty on the part of the children toward parents. This also led to the fact that the children began to view the parents as unresponsive and irresponsible. J is aware of the lack of social solidarity between parents and children. He says in J4: ". . . if we as parents did what they did thirty years ago there would have been more positive changes in this country by now." This absence of solidarity between children and parents is not conducive towards parental responsibility and responsiveness.

The Story of Mr. D.

Psychological Interpretation

The theme of "intimacy vs. isolation" relates to Mr. D's earlier days as a child. In those days, about 50 or 60 years ago, blacks and whites "lived together" (D1). The apartheid laws that came into effect in 1948 brought about enforced isolation between blacks and whites. This led to stagnation in race relations and in human existence as a whole in South Africa. "The blacks were pushed to the sideline because Afrikaners wanted to be a 'pure race' like the nazis" (D1). Here we are dealing with Erikson's concept of pseudospeciation which refers to the fact that a particular group views themselves as the human species. All others are excluded from this classification.[10] The "Group Areas Act" brought about further stagnation and a reinforcement of the "Isolation Theme." By means of this law the South African government forced each ethnic group to live in residential areas designated as such by law.

The theme of "generativity vs. stagnation" is reflected in a rather harsh way in D's upbringing as a child. It was in order for another adult to spank someone else's child if that child stepped out of line. "There was respect and discipline....Our parents were so strict..." (D2). Generativity was carried out in a very authoritarian manner by the parents of that day.

Our theme of "generativity vs. stagnation" is also reflected in the way that Mr. D views present day children. He seems to expect the same kind of response to parental authoritarianism that he experienced as a child. But this kind of caring for children has been disrupted by the current generation of young people. For Mr. D the result is stagnation in his relationship with his children. He says: "But today kids have no respect for their parents" (D2). He seems to forget that his children may be reflecting his actions as a young person: "I was wild in my young days" (D2).

Identity formation in young people in Mr. D's childhood days was intricately interwoven with the ideology of religion. Religious values greatly affected the child-parent relationships of that time (D2). But times have changed. The crisis situation in South Africa is taking place in a pluralistic context in which children have to grapple with foreign ideologies that dominate their social environment, e.g., marxism. A radical monotheistic faith in the One universal God is being challenged by henotheism. The accompanying tensions of the latter with the strained parent-child relationships lead to stagnation in the caring of people like Mr. D toward his children.

Mr. D declares that the apartheid laws have a limiting effect on his parenting abilities. He refers to his experience with his children at the Cango Caves in Oudshoorn, South Africa, and taking his children to the beach. On both occasions they were confronted by segregation (D3). He relates how difficult it was for him as a parent to take his children through those humiliating experiences. He was very conscious of the limiting effects of apartheid on his parenting powers at that time. A feeling of stagnation prevailed then.

While Mr. D would encourage his children to fight for their rights one detects an element of fear about the method that these children are using to achieve those rights. With these thoughts that he relates in D4 he conveys the distinct impression that it is hard to care for one's child in a crisis situation like that which prevails in South Africa.

Ethical Interpretation

When Mr. D's childhood experiences are related to Niebuhr's dynamic faith triad one becomes aware of the fact that initially there was a state of harmony in the triad relationshipwise. "...In those days whites and blacks lived together." Responsiveness between the self (Mr. D) and other selves (white people) as well as responsibility was more positive then. But, in 1948 the pattern of interrelationships in the triad was disrupted with the advent of apartheid. Mr. D's story sheds more light on the responsibility of black South African adults when it is viewed in the light of the various elements that constitute Niebuhr's responsibility ethics.

1. *Response*: Psychologically and in his memory Mr. D has a degree of connectedness with his parents. He must have interiorized their values and authoritarian forms of discipline. If, as appears to the case, this shaped his own generative pattern then it would be inevitable for a strong element of irresponsibility to prevail in his actions. Outside the home, e.g., on the trip to the Cango Caves and to the beach, Mr. D responded to his kids in a deontological fashion, that is, with the law in mind. He had no alternative but to respond to the two situations in question the way the law dictated to him.

2. *Interpretation*: When Mr. D asks himself the question, What is happening?, he is confronted by the forces of stagnation that dominate his world, e.g., an oppressive government. In response to the two doors labelled "whites" and "non-whites" he says: "How stupid can you get" (D3). This is a response of anger, bitterness, and resentment. This response could also be interpreted as a stagnant response because the effects it will have will not be positive. It will not have a healthy effect on his existence as a relational person. In his responsibility towards his children he interprets their existence in a horizontal fashion which puts it in a wider perspective that transcends the narrow confines of a deontological interpretation. He says: "I say to every youth: Fight for your rights. You have rights which God gave to all his people" (D4). However, he is

concerned about the way in which they are going about getting their rights,e.g., the school boycotts and the stone throwing.

3. *Accountability*: The element of accountability as it operates in the response pattern of Mr. D prevents him from being fully responsible. If we take two incidents into consideration we notice that Mr. D did have expectations of certain reactions to responses that he executed or would execute in those situations. There was also a sense of judgment that was implied in those responses.

The first incident occurred at the Cango Caves (D3). Mr. D knew that if he deliberately entered the Cango Caves through the "whites only" entrance he and his children would be prosecuted. He could also expect protests and resentment from the white tourists. He would have liked to respond to the degrading apartheid signs with defiance. However, because he had expectations of the kind of hostile responses that he would receive he chose to respond under the pressures of the imposed limitations. Thus his judgment warned him of impending harm to him and his children and thus he responded in the latter way. The same expectations, pattern of response, and implied judgment prevailed when he took his children to a segregated beach.

4. *Social Solidarity*: Mr. D is subconsciously aware of the fact that his responses are part of a continuous process of responses that occurred before him and would also occur in the future unless the pattern of limitations on his actions and the pattern of responsibility is disrupted and replaced by a process of reconciliation. Black adults before him were subjected to the same limitations, self-imposed irresponsibility and anticipations of reactions to gut reactions in the subconscious. He is aware of the fact that what he is experiencing with his children is taking place in an oppressive social context which makes him to experience a sense of powerlessness.

The Story of Mr. E.

Psychological Interpretation

The theme of "intimacy vs. isolation" is presented as we focus on Mr. E's early childhood years. He says: "I had happy childhood years near our church..." (E1). But this sense of intimacy with a happy environment, family home, neighborhood friends, and beloved church was rudely disrupted by the imposition of the "Group Areas Act," which forced them out of an area that they loved deeply. The theme of "trust vs. mistrust" is then reflected in the words: "I did not understand very well but it made a very vivid impression on my mind. We had to make new friends . . ." (E1). The government sowed seeds of mistrust towards white people in a sensitive black mind as well as the seeds of hostility, rebellion, and perhaps hatred towards an "enemy" who was unfair.

Through its Group Areas Act the South African government literally forced black people (E's family) and others like them to experience an enforced form of intimacy. Here we notice an enforced version of the "intimacy vs. isolation" theme which is really a theme of stagnation. When he completed high school E once again experienced a disruption of the "intimacy vs. isolation" theme when they were forced to leave an area where they were forced to live by law. The "trust vs. mistrust" theme, particularly towards a hostile government and towards black people, prevailed once more.

During his senior year at high school he committed his life to Christ. On this level he experienced the highest form of intimacy, that is, with God (E1). His joining the Christian Institute also gave him another sense of intimacy. In E1 he expresses this isolation in a very acute way when he utters that he was robbed of his roots (E1). The discovery of Christ in his life probably countered the stagnation that he experienced on numerous occasions.

In E2 we detect how difficult it is to be generative to his child in a "militarized society." E gives the impression that generativity is greatly curtailed in such an environment. He finds it hard to be generative towards his child in an environment where his five-year old has to be filled with fear and "to run into our house when the police approach because his friends have said to him...the police kill children" (E2).

When he relates the story of the arrest of the 22 black youths (students) by the police during the state of unrest in the country he is relating the core experience of every black adult with children in South Africa. He mentions the fear of the police, the terror, the sense of helplessness when one's children are arrested. What he is sharing is the theme of "generativity vs. stagnation," experienced by black South African adults in an acute crisis situation.

Ethical Interpretation

Early in his life E's parents were forced to respond in a deontological fashion to oppressive and limiting forces. When they were forced out of their home his parents had to respond to a law that was inhuman and harsh. "...It made a vivid impression on my mind" (E1). They were forced to leave their home twice under the Group Areas Act. This caused the young E to question the responses of the dominant forces in his country: "I asked myself the question: Why should black people be chased out of their homes every time?" In a sense he could have been asking: "Why should my parents be forced to be unresponsive every time in the face of such inhumane treatment?" It is inevitable that the young E would have interiorized this unresponsiveness of his parents towards the government, the police, and the army who did just as they pleased. When we bring the elements of responsibility into focus in E's life we become aware of many dynamics.

1. *Response*: Because of a strong deontological context in which they lived E's parents were forced to be unresponsive to a large degree. This was transferred to E. When he became an adult he was subjected to the same deontological context when he became unresponsive towards the laws of his land and experienced limitations as he tried to raise his child under apartheid. Unresponsiveness is thus a vicious cycle in his family like it is in many black families. This situation does not arise by choice though.

2. *Interpretation*: This element of responsibility suggests the dynamic of freedom. This is a freedom which helps the agent to decide on what kind of response he wants executed. Interpretation helps the individual to make a fitting response. How does E respond to actions that come down upon him? In E1 he had no alternative but to respond to a limiting situation, that is, eviction from their home by the Groups Areas Act, the same say his parents did. They were forced to move. It may not have been the proper decision to take and the proper response to make from the standpoint of human dignity but it was "the most appropriate one under the circumstances that prevailed."

His commitment to Christ during his senior high school years was a very positive response to all the actions both positive and negative that came upon him. However, he mentions in E1 that he responded negatively towards a major chapter in his life, that is, when he was robbed of his roots by the Group Areas Act. He thus made an interpretation here to a situation which he regarded as stagnant.

Under E2 we detect E's difficulty in interpreting a militarized situation to his son. This difficulty in interpretation makes response and responsibility an arduous task. In spite of all the debilitating forces in his society he nevertheless tries to let the Word of God interpret situations to his congregation. But the reality of the South African situation remains a hard and painful one for blacks. By letting the Word interpret he tries to keep the "Center of Value" where it belongs, that is, at the fulcrum of the Christian life.

Under E3 we view E's interpretation from another angle. His interpretation of apartheid is that it is bad and has a negative effect on him. "This system wants to play God." The only alternative that he is left with is to respond negatively toward it. "Apartheid limits one in everything that one does. It prevents one from being a parent..."(E3). With this latter statement E suggests that apartheid causes a black parent to be irresponsible by deliberately limiting their ability to take action on a moral and ethical level. "The child who has to look up to that parent sees how powerless that parent is" (E3). This latter statement reinforces a spirit of unresponsiveness and irresponsibility in the child. At the same time it causes tension in the parent-child relationship because the child becomes confused when it sees its role model and hero delegitimatized and treated disrespectfully.

3. *Accountability*: Jerry Irish, an interpreter of Niebuhr, says: "Accountability is another way of posing the question, 'To whom or what am I responding and in what context?'"[11]   It is obvious that E is responding to an oppressive situation that has a limiting effect on him and his child. He has certain expectations of reactions to his responses. Subconsciously he knows that if he responds to those limiting situations that are confronting him according to the dictation of his conscience then he would meet with negative reactions. The context to which he is responding is one which causes him to experience a sense of powerlessness and unresponsiveness. As far as his accountability is concerned he realizes that some responses are more fitting than others. Thus he responds in a "safe" way. In the context of the dynamic faith triad this type of action is really irresponsible action as he is not being true to himself by responding in this way.

4. *Social Solidarity*: E is part of a community of selves. This gives him a sense of connectedness with the "other selves" in the faith triad. While E's responses are to a certain degree regarded as irresponsible it could be viewed as responsible in the context of interaction with other selves. In this latter case we include the South African government, their army, and police as part of the network of "other selves." When viewed in this light E's responses are not as distorted as they appear to be when viewed from a very narrow angle of partial responsibility. When E's actions are furthermore viewed in the national South African context of social solidarity they cannot be labelled as peculiar to him alone. On a generational level he is part of a social solidarity network. By this we mean that his grandparents acted the way he does and so did his parents when confronted by limiting forces. Under the heading of social solidarity as a partial instrument for measuring responsibility Jerry Irish states the following: "In order for a response to be fitting it must fit into what is actually going on."[12] E's response to various actions upon him may thus be regarded as fitting or responsible response because it fits what is going on, namely, actions in a stagnant, limiting situation.

General Summary of the Five Cases

Analysis of the five stories in light of our ethical-psychological model reveals the following. Certain ethical and psychological themes are more prominent than others. But together all of these shed light on the psychological and ethical dynamics of generativity vs. stagnation and irresponsibility vs. responsibility as they operate in the lives of black adults in South Africa. It is important to mention that by irresponsibility in the context of our analysis of our five cases we mean the lack of or inability to care for someone.

Psychological

From the perspective of Erikson's psychosocial theory all the adults interviewed experience problems with their youth in the context of various themes. These are the main ones:

Trust vs. Mistrust: Many young people have questions in their minds as to whether they can really trust their parents to support them fully in their "struggle for freedom" from the yoke of apartheid. The majority of them experience doubt in this regard. They cannot appreciate the fact that their parents are motivated primarily to protect them from imprisonment and death. To them the latter are secondary concerns. Most of the children of the parents interviewed do not trust the religious ideology of their parents. In the latter case we are referring to a radical monotheistic faith in the one universal God of the Bible which conflicts with the most appealing and "relevant" ideology of marxism.

Identity vs. Role Confusion: The young people notice that their role models, their parents, are unsure of their roles and responses in the current crisis situation. They are also aware of the fact that the limitations that the South African government with the aid of their laws impose upon them and force them to be "irresponsible and ungenerative." This causes acute identity confusion in the psyches of these young people coupled to the other developmental problems that they are experiencing in their quest for an identity of their own.   Thus, our ethical-psychological model as an instrument of analysis could be used as a tool to enable black adults to become more aware of problems like the above and assist them to transcend them. In this way our model could contribute towards the counteracting of stagnation.

Intimacy vs. isolation: This theme dominates in a powerful way in the story of all our interviewees. Problems with trust vs. mistrust and identity vs. identity confusion, to mention two examples, contribute to the prominence of the intimacy vs. isolation theme. The above have created a hiatus in the parent-child relationships among blacks in South Africa. They are not the only causes of this hiatus though. As the crisis in South Africa escalates from day to day greater isolation is experienced by both parents and youth towards each other as the mistrust, identity confusion, etc., grow bigger. Our model can aid in the analysis and interpretation of this problem and bring about a process that could lead to trust, identity, and greater intimacy between black adults and their youth.

Erikson points out that the basis of developmental issues is the epigenetic principle (discussed in chapter 1 of this book). In other words, the problem did not just happen but it evolved through a series of stages from the foundation of a ground plan. Critical steps occurred along the route of the life cycle. By critical we mean a number of turning points or moments of decision between progress and regression, integration and retardation.[13] All people have the "capacity over time to change and grow."[14] It is our aim with the aid of our ethical-psychological model to achieve this, to enable black adults to become generative.

Ethical

On the ethical level it would be unfair to state that all our adults who were interviewed are totally "irresponsible." Our instruments of analysis have indicated, from the perspective of responsibility, that the adults in question revealed strengths on the basis of one or more of the elements of responsibility, e.g., some were more accountable, more aware of their social solidarity, or more responsible than others. However, it became clear that the limitations imposed by South African society do curb the parenting functions of these parents from an ethical point of view rendering their range for ethical action defective, inappropriate, and partially irresponsible.

An acute crisis has evolved as far as "The Center of Value" which is intricately interwoven with a radical monotheistic faith is concerned. The center of value in Christian homes is gradually but surely being shoved to the periphery of Christian family life in the black community in South Africa. This in turn has a detrimental effect on Christian values that formed the backbone for morality and ethics in these homes for generations. This is also coupled with an ideological struggle in black homes as the hearts and minds of many black youth are being conquered by marxism.

A self responds with loyalty and commitment to a cause. In the case of young people this takes on a much more acute form than in adults as it is part of their developmental struggle to achieve an identity. Our model could contribute towards aiding black adults to interpret the context of their parent-child struggles with a sober and balanced frame of mind. This in turn could hopefully enable them to give their children a relevant cause to which they could pledge their loyalty and commitment. In this regard we are referring to a commitment and loyalty to the One God beyond the many in a pluralistic society. The cause usually transcends the self and has the power to transform it. If self-transformation could be achieved in both parents and children in our situation the goal of responsibility and generativity becomes a real possibility.

Niebuhr says that the understanding of the self and the way it responds can only be comprehended in relation to a value center. For Niebuhr and for every Christian this value center is God. When the self has a clear identity (reference to both black adults and black youth) they will have a solid foundation to stand on and a secure base from which to relate to each other. From a Niebuhrian perspective this base is a monotheistic faith in God. From an Eriksonian perspective this base is identity. Then all the elements of the responsibility theory--response, accountability, interpretation, and social solidarity--could function together in a synchronized and harmonious way. Furthermore, both parties could ask with more boldness in response to actions that come onto them: "What is happening?" This question could then be anticipated with a divine answer received in faith, namely: God is acting on me in every circumstance that comes my way. Therefore I can respond to everything that is happening to me as if I am responding to God. Finally there will be harmony between the three points of the Triad when this occurs, namely, between God, Self, and Other Selves.

CHAPTER 5

IMPLICATIONS FOR PASTORAL CARE IN SOUTH AFRICA

The relationship between Niebuhr's Ethics of Responsibility and Erikson's Psychosocial Theory point to a strong connectedness between psychology and theological ethics. This connectedness indicates that human beings could be viewed from a number of perspectives. In this case that perspective is ethical-psychological in nature. This means that people possess both ethical and psychological qualities. These are not the only qualities that they possess though. By psychological we mean the emotional and interpersonal dynamics in the inner life of a person. Ethical in this regard refers to dynamics that are related to normative value symbols and the moral structures that guide our lives. These insights gave rise to the construction of an ethical-psychological model that could be employed in the rendering of pastoral care to black adults in South Africa.

The conclusion that is drawn is that a relationship does exist between responsibility and generativity and that they are particularly strongly linked at two points that are common to them, namely faith and identity. The correlation between them has been pointed out (chapter 3). This responsibility-generativity relationship has far-reaching implications for the execution of pastoral care towards black adults in South Africa. In chapter 4 it was determined that black adults are *not* fully responsible/ responsive and fully generative towards their youth. There is present a degree of responsibility/responsiveness and generativity though. However, this causes the quality of care to their youth to be impoverished due to the fact that their range for ethical action is severely curtailed by the society in which they exist. With this book we are now able to make a contribution towards remedying this situation in the context of pastoral care. This is, however, not the only way of remedying the situation. To be more specific, we want to engage our ethical-psychological model to achieve this.

The dynamics inherent in the relationship that exists between responsibility and generativity, together with our model, have far-reaching implications for the rendering of pastoral care to black adults in South Africa. The latter group of individuals are in need of a relevant pastoral care to assist them as they grapple with various problems, in particular problems of faith and identity. The latter form the connecting point for the issues of responsibility and generativity. We propose to focus on these implications in the following way or from the following perspectives:

1.   Black South Africans as "Living Human Documents" (ethical-psychological documents).   In this regard we will draw heavily upon Charles Gerkin's book, *The Living Human Document* (Revisioning Pastoral Counseling in a Hermeneutical Mode).   Gerkin in turn draws on Anton Boison's image of "the living human document."

The procedure we want to follow in this regard is to sketch the implications of our study for pastoral care to black adults in the light of our ethical-psychological model. This will be done by channeling this model through the image of these adults as living human documents (ethical-psychological documents).

2. Second, we will employ Hans-George Gadamer, the Heidelberg philosopher's simile of the Fusion of Horizons (intersubjectivity).

3. Donald Capps' ideas on pastoral care and life cycle theory as expounded in his book, *Life Cycle Theory and Pastoral Care*.[1]

4.   Finally Don Browning's ideas on the *Moral Context of Pastoral Care* as expounded in his book.[2]

A. *The Image of the Living Human Document*

The "Living Human Document" is the central image in Anton Boison's work, *The Exploration of the Inner World*. It enables us to understand the implications of our ethical-psychological model for black adults in South Africa as follows: Boison says that this text can "become confused" at times:

> Something has happened which has upset the foundations upon which his ordinary reasoning is based.[3]

During such periods the "living human document" needs an interpreter and a guide.[4] Furthermore, it is at such a point that our ethical-psychological model could be employed by the pastor to reflect on and to interpret the chaos and confusion in the text of troubled black adults.   To understand the ungenerative and irresponsible/ irresponsive behavior of black adults in South Africa is a hermeneutical task.   Our model could be regarded as a hermeneutical model as it interprets human (black adult) experience by means of psychological/ethical language and insights. This in turn connects experience (that of generativity and responsibility) to language, giving meaning to that experience. Dilthey[5] suggests that in order to understand another means to grasp the mind of that other, the inner world of that person.   Gerkin, drawing on Dilthey's thoughts, says that "...all understanding of human experience is fundamentally historical; meaning and meaninglessness are contextual.   They emerge from the situation of a time and place.[6]   In this regard I want to suggest that from a pastoral care perspective the context referred to above, in the case of the black South African adult, is a moral one which is much deeper and larger than the one currently and traditionally used by black pastors in South Africa.

Many black adults in South Africa have become so conditioned by the values of the dominant minority that they socialize their children on the basis of standards, norms, values, and a concept of reality laid down by the above minority. Too much blame should not be put on such adults as they were probably socialized in the same way by their parents. This thought just highlights the need for an effective instrument in pastoral care to break a generational cycle of psychological and moral stagnation. The internalization of values, norms, and distorted concepts of reality referred to above greatly contribute to the formation of identity confusion in black youth in South Africa, as well as to negative self-concepts.

The realm of faith has also been complicated by the above internalizations. Faith forms a central part of the black South African's philosophy of life. When white society in South Africa colors the Divine with caucasian features and mannerisms it leads to a faith crisis in blacks, particularly the youth. It has come to light that these young people are increasingly questioning the attributes of a god with whom they cannot identify. This creates another problematic avenue for personality development among blacks, e.g., despising the self and confusion due to the fact that they are forced to approximate white appearances as closely as possible in a society that despises their God-given attributes. This in turn shapes and inhibits their responsiveness and responsibility toward their environment and those with whom they interact in it in a negative way. Black South African youth are also socialized very early in life by societal institutions, e.g., schools and in some cases the church to accept the imposed limitations to their existence as human beings.

> He comes to understand that to challenge the
> definition the others have given him will destroy

> him.   It is impressed upon him that the
> incompetent, acquiescent, and irrespon-
> sible...survives while the competent, aggressive
> black is systematically suppressed.[7]

These are the seeds of what Erikson calls identity confusion that will be transferred to adulthood from the basic structure of an irresponsible/unresponsive personality. This distorted self-concept has a detrimental effect on the negotiation of the stages of the life cycle that follow (in this case adolescence).   Subsequently they affect the ethical actions of the evolving black adult in a detrimental way.   I want to suggest that most black adults in South Africa socialize their children sub-consciously to conform to the standards of white society in that country to ensure their survival. This is their way of caring for them in a stagnant society.   But at the same time many of them neglect to impress upon these youth the importance of interpreting the negative dynamics of this socialization process of the dominant minority to ensure this survival and the avoidance of punitive measures by society for "stepping out of bounds."   The black child thus indirectly is not encouraged to be aggressive and assertive in a positive way by their parents and society. Such attitudes are necessary to enable them to compete on an equal footing with all people in the world at large. This negligence is based on deeply ingrained fears of reprisals against socialization processes that try to instill *full* generativity and *full* responsibility and responsiveness in the youth.

Black South African adults have been forced to grow up with certain stigmas since their childhood days. These stigmas have given rise to the fact that many of them have become psychologically embedded in mistrust, self-doubt, shame (of their color, for example), and isolation and alienation. Erving Goffman says:

Further, the standards he has incorporated from
the wider society equip him to be intimately alive
to what others see as his failing, inevitably
causing him, if only for moments, to agree that he
does indeed fall short of what he really ought to
be. Shame becomes a central possibility....[8]

Erikson gives us a vivid explanation of the negative
effects of shame on the personality.[9] Shame and doubt go
together. Autonomy vs. shame and doubt is the crisis which
the ego has to resolve in the second stage. I believe that
many black adults experience fixation in shame and doubt
and perhaps also in mistrust and stagnation. These cause
further psychological problems insofar as the "cogwheeling
relationships" between the life cycles of black adults and
their younger generation is concerned. These youth
subconsciously internalize a stigma theory like that which
is internalized by their parents. And eventually these form
the foundation for psychosocial stagnation, ungenerativity,
and unresponsiveness/irresponsibility in later years.
Goffman says:

By definition, of course, we believe the person
with a stigma is not quite human. On this
assumption (the dominant group in society)
exercise varieties of discrimination, through
which we effectively, if often unthinkingly, reduce
his life chances. We construct a stigma theory,
an ideology to explain his inferiority and account
for the danger he presents, sometimes
rationalizing an animosity based on other
differences, such as that of class.[10]

The political realities of the South African situation
cause the intergenerational problem between black adults
and youth to be complicated even further. The fact of the
matter is that a whole generation of black youth are
growing up at present in South African struggling with the

repercussions of violent conflict and violence as that country slips further into a deepening civil crisis. It is a violence that leaves very little room for them to work through the crisis and problems of adolescence. This has a detrimental effect on their personalities and causes regression in many cases. My hunch is that we may see a whole future generation of black adults suffering from fixation in the adolescent stage. This will contribute further toward the evolvement of stagnation, unresponsiveness, and irresponsibility in the ensuing generation.

Erikson's theory states that stagnation or ungenerativity can only be eradicated when generativity outweighs stagnation in the adult stage. The implication of this fact for pastoral care is that black adults will only be able to care fully for their youth and give them a clear and positive identity when they are aided to overcome stagnation and irresponsibility by means of our model.

In order to be relevant these pastors should not overlook the fact that the problems of these troubled individuals have a moral context. If the language of that disturbed personal universe is tinted with a value and normative-laden vocabulary the pastor should be able to detect the signal that is indicating the way for the engagement of our model to restore meaning to that world. This image of the pastoral care seeker as an ethical-psychological document opens up new possibilities for the South African pastor to come to grips with the need of restoring pastoral care to a position of relevance for his people. Our model may prove to be the most effective instrument to achieve this.

Gerkin says: "To speak of the person as a living document is to acknowledge this connection between life and language. It is to acknowledge that to understand what Boison calls the inner world is dependent upon understanding the language by which that inner world of experience is connected to external events. To understand

the inner world of another is therefore a task of interpretation--interpretation of a world of experience...."[11]
For the South African situation this implies that the irresponsible/unresponsive and ungenerative black adult will express his "inner world of experience" more strongly in ethical, value-laden terms as well as in psychological language (than in any other), which could be interpreted by means of our model which is a hermeneutical-ethical-psychological instrument. These ethical-psychological languages run parallel at first but they merge at a point where they meet a transcendent factor. This is the point at which Niebuhr's ethics and his theological language as it is related to God, the transcendent One, must be employed, as well as acting as a corrective to psychological theories. An event only becomes an experience when it is linked to a language.[12] The ethical (theological) psychological language of our model has a strong connection with the experience of the inner world of ungenerativity and unresponsiveness/irresponsibility of the adults under discussion.It is right at this point that the language world out of which the

> pastoral counselor shapes his perceptions and response to the other person becomes crucial. If that be a language world inhabited by the images of faith and theology [and ethics], the counselee will be invited into a world shaped by those images. (brackets mine)[13]

Implicit in these words is a pastoral invitation to the ungenerative and irresponsible/unresponsive individual in South Africa to enter an empathic world, a world with a moral context in which the core of the dislocation of that inner world will be addressed and a relevant attempt made to restore the imbalance in the human condition that is located there. Gerkin finds it helpful to turn to Gadamer

for reinforcement of his hermeneutical position. Let us turn
to Gadamer's thoughts on this matter.

B. *Gadamer's Idea of the Fusion of Horizons*

Drawing upon Gadamer, Gerkin emphasizes the fact
that another important hermeneutical perspective is the
"horizon of understanding." According to Gadamer, due to
the fact that one is part of a historical pattern a
hermeneutical action cannot occur on a subject-object
basis.[14] In other words, one cannot make a study of the
history of a particular person when one is positioned outside
the ambit of that history,[15] or, e.g., if one stands outside the
ethical-psychological-moral dynamics of the careseeker's
horizon. Gadamer declares that hermeneutics can only take
place on a dialogical basis.[16] This thought is harmonious
with Niebuhr's thoughts on the relational existence of the
self with other selves and God on a dialogical basis. In such
a context the inner world of the interpreter becomes fused
with and merges with that of the text. Only on the above
basis can there be a fusion of horizons of meaning and
understanding.[17]

This point is crucial for the execution of pastoral
care to black adults in South Africa. For such pastoral care
to be effective the above point implies that the pastor should
merge his horizon, in particular the repressed
ethical-psychological dimension of that horizon, with similar
dimensions that he boldly recognizes in the horizon of the
helpseeker. This is the only way in which he will get into
that person's horizon/text, and inner life in order to
understand their ungenerativity and irresponsibility/
unresponsiveness and the wider moral implications thereof.
This would allow a relevant dialogue to take place between
pastor and pastoral care receiver on the basis of a strong
common moral denominator.

In Niebuhrian terms the interaction that is taking place here occurs in a triadic relationship which could be explained as follows: In a pastoral care situation an engagement or fusion occurs between two horizons, namely that of the pastor and that of the pastoral care receiver. This fusion will bring about the experience of tension between the latter two. The existence of this tension should not be denied.[18] If a denial occurs the hermeneutical task of the pastor will become impoverished. Consequently he would be unable to come to grips with the hurt and suffering that is part of the imbalance in the human condition of the careseeker.

During this pastoral care/pastoral counseling event a disclosure occurs which is also a transformation event. A new revelation comes out of this fusion of two horizons. This transformation event, this revelation, is God, who enters this diadic relationship to make it a triadic one that takes on new depth, and new meaning particularly for the counselee. This in turn opens the way for the rendering of more effective pastoral care. This fusion will occur with a divine power that includes, yet overshadows, ethics and psychology.   His is a horizon of faith, grace, and empowerment which is also generative, responsive, and responsible. This can only take place when there is an openness on the part of both pastor and pastoral care receiver. In this moment change will occur in both.[19]

Many black pastors in South Africa have made themselves guilty of a subject-object form of counseling and pastoral caring. In the light of Niebuhr's triad of faith this would minimize the influence of the third factor in the triad, the most important one, namely God, and the connection between responsibility, generativity, and God. Only when there is a true fusion of horizons between pastor, care receiver, and God can the true fusion of horizons between pastor, care receiver, and theirs with God take place. Similarly, only in this manner can the true relationship between responsibility and generativity come to the fore.

This in turn will highlight the moral context in which this pastoral care that leads to an increase in responsibility and generativity take place.

A further implication of Gadamer's image of understanding on the basis of an intersubjective merger of horizons is that it acts as a corrective to Hiltner's eductive approach to counseling and pastoral care. It also acts as a corrective for the purely spiritual and biblicistic approach to pastoral care of the black pastor in South Africa. Hiltner refers to *eductive* as that part of the shepherding perspective that "leads out" elements that are inside a pastoral care receiver or may be potentially available to him.[20]

Gerkin referring to Gadamer says:

> It breaks apart the understanding of pastoral care and counseling as involving primarily the application of learned techniques to the solving of human problems...care and counseling considered as a hermeneutical process.... In Gadamer's language, the "text" must be allowed to tell the pastor something, "to assert its own truth against one's foremeanings."[21]

In view of the fact that the relationship between responsibility and generativity has been established black pastors should be encouraged to utilize the model in the reconstruction of black adult-youth relationships. In this regard I wish to highlight the following two main points, namely: black parents could be given a new image in the eyes of their children and vice versa. Our model could give them greater insights into the evolvement of their personalities as well as better comprehension of psychodynamics like identity confusion in the lives of their youth. Also, from an ethical angle they could obtain a better grasp of their responsibility and responsiveness personally and in a society that inhibits it. The latter could be brought about as a result of the metaphor of the Responsible Self acting as a key to self-analysis from an ethical perspective.

It is thus fair to conclude that black adults in South Africa are not ungenerative, irresponsible, and unresponsive to a degree by choice but due to the stagnant forces in the context of their existence. This context contains threats and dynamics that create fear, anxiety, mistrust, and despair in their psyches and in the black family system. This in turn creates intergenerational conflict and forces these adults to place greater emphasis on the survival and protection of their children. The end result is inevitably ungenerativity and irresponsibility. Our model clearly indicates that these two issues are symptomatic of negative dynamics in the unconscious of these adults. This model could enable the pastor to focus on the total human being by bringing to his awareness the psychological, ethical, and theological dimensions of human response to situations.

We have established that the life cycle of the black adult is embedded in a social context which is much larger than the narrow spiritual context traditionally focused on by pastors in South Africa. Human development, according to Erikson, proceeds by stages. The implication is that if a stage is poorly negotiated due to, among others, a poor negotiation of a prior stage adequate progress will not be discerned in the ensuing stages. For this thought and those that follow I am indebted to Donald Capps and his book, *Life Cycle and Pastoral Care.*[22]

C. *Life Cycle Theory and Pastoral Care (Capps)*

Acceleration of the stages could also occur due to the context of people's existence, e.g., in South Africa the stages of the life cycle of black children appear to be moving more rapidly than should be the case due to the fact that they have been forced to confront adult psycho-ethical issues and dynamics that usually occur in the adult stages of the life cycle at very tender ages. To put it another way, black children have been forced to respond like adults to adult issues that they are faced with while biologically and psychoethically they may not be adequately prepared for it.

1. *Regression and Acceleration:* In the adult regression could take place when a sense of generativity has been lost.[23] Erikson suggests that earlier stages may be experienced again.[24] I want to suggest that black adults in South Africa regress to earlier stages to re-experience lost trust, autonomy, identity, etc. In the same vein I want to suggest that the black youth accelerate, at times, to later stages to make up subconsciously for that which they sense their parents have lost. This symbiotic pattern could possibly be brought about by the fact that the life cycles of adults and children exist in a "cogwheeling" relationship.

2. *Epigenesis:* From an epigenetic point of view Erikson's theory shows that a negative environment could have a detrimental effect on the growth of an individual at any stage of the life cycle.[25] Our model could enable the pastor to respond in a relevant and dynamic way to those forces which create an imbalance in the environment of the troubled person. Furthermore, the psychological dimension of our model could assist the pastor to address issues like trust-mistrust, shame, intimacy, isolation and identity confusion. All of these have an effect on generativity which is an ethical stage in Erikson's theory.

3. *Virtues, Responsibility, and Encounter:* Erikson's schedule of virtues and Niebuhr's understanding of responsibility in the individual also blend nicely. Capps says, "Erikson thinks of these virtues not as static traits but as inherent strengths that are cultivated in encounter. They become alive and vital through our interaction with persons and social institutions, especially those most

decisively involved in our lives at that developmental
stage....We need to recognize that the virtues are linked to
developmental stages. If this is not understood, our efforts
to inspire virtue in our children and cultivate virtue in
ourselves will be haphazard and arbitrary."[26]

This excellent interpretation of a vital aspect of
Erikson's theory suggests that there is a parallel with
Niebuhr's idea of responsibility in this regard. The parent
who has been enabled to be responsible through encounter
(or relational existence) in the context of the triad of faith
(Niebuhr) would enable his child to be responsible via the
"cogwheeling" process. By means of responsible encounter
the cultivation of virtues which are vital for the development of an ethical sense will be given a boost.

Another implication for our study is the fact that
there are certain attitudes behind the issues of ungenerativity and irresponsibility. These attitudes could be
illustrated by means of vices which "hinder our efforts to
give moral order to our lives."[27]

What Capps refers to as vices Erikson prefers to
refer to as pathological antipathies.

4. *Pathological Antipathies:* These antipathies are:
withdrawal, compulsion, inhibition, inertia, repudiation,
exclusivity, rejectivity, and disdain. We shall only refer to
rejectivity in the following paragraph. According to Erikson
an antipathy occurs at every stage of the life cycle and they
are in disharmony with the virtues of that particular stage.
Let us focus for a moment on the virtue of care which is
crucial for the understanding of the issue of generativity.
Care is the strength or virtue which arises at this stage.
Erikson says:

> If care (as all other strengths cited) is the
> expression of a vital sympathetic trend with a
> high instinctual energy at its disposal, there is
> also a corresponding antipathetic trend...in the

> stage of generativity, it is rejectivity; that is, the
> unwillingness to include specific persons or
> groups in one's generative concern--one does not
> care for them[28]

Capps warns that these vices should be viewed in a serious light as they have a powerful effect on the way in which our moral character is molded.[29] I want to suggest that the stagnant and immoral societal context in South Africa reinforces the development of these in black South Africans. The best way in which these could be curtailed is for the pastor to be attentive to the way in which Erikson's theory clarifies this dilemma for him. This clarification should be shared with the care receiver to empower him to face and overcome this problem. Similarly, when this dilemma is approached from a responsibility perspective the pastor should allow the dynamics inherent in his and the care receiver's response to the ground of their being which is God, to be the pattern and force that will inform the moral approach to these antipathies. Broadly put, the pastor should guide the person to respond first to an encounter with the One who is the shaper of all moral behavior, the one who can eradicate all antipathies with his generative power of love, grace, redemption, and reconciliation, namely God.

Capps indicates how hope could counter the antipathy of gluttony.[30] This point is helpful for the flow of the above discussion. "If we have real hope we do not fear for the future, and therefore we do not need to secure an overabundance of supplies in the here and now.[31] This thought of Capps could be applied in an analogous way to stagnation or ungenerativity. Stagnation can take various forms, e.g., lack of care, gluttony, a relationship devoid of love or intimacy, pseudospeciation, etc. Informed by Erikson's theory the pastor could lead the careseeker to an experience of hope in the source of all hope, God. This kind of experience of God could strengthen generativity and give the black South African adult a new way of being generative and responsible through Christ. The careseeker could also be brought to an awareness that he need not have "abundant supplies" of self-absorption and ungenerativity, employed as defense mechanisms against overpowering and limiting forces of stagnation. The mistrust that accompanies stagnation also accompanies irresponsibility and unresponsiveness. If the pastor enables the careseeker, with the aid of our instrument of analysis and hermeneutical model, to respond as if they are responding to God, the source of hope and trust (Niebuhr), he could enable them to break out of embeddedness in unresponsiveness and irresponsibility. And this in turn could empower them to face the future with peace and boldness.

In this way the pastor could use his psycho-moral-ethical skills to restore a degree of moral-ethical balance to a situation that is in a state of moral-ethical imbalance. In this way the pastor will avoid being a mere personal comforter but a moral counselor.

The developmental nature of Erikson's theory and the developmental nature to a lesser degree of Niebuhr's ethics of responsibility could also inform the South African pastor's method of caregiving. When the antipathy of rejectivity in the generativity vs. stagnation stage has been overcome these adults could be empowered to cope with another societal force, namely *limitations*. These societal limitations resist generativity and responsibility. The ethical dimension of the model would be most effective here. What do we mean by this?

In the light of Niebuhr's ethics black adults could use the symbol of the responsible self to counter limitations imposed upon them. How? Niebuhr could aid them to interpret these powers (e.g., the South African laws and prejudiced people) as powers that are not autonomous but under the direction and guidance of God. This is the way

Niebuhr views the limiting powers of Pilate upon Jesus. In the context of responsible ethics Pilate was not an autonomous power but an individual under God's divine influence.[32] Subsequently they would see that "...pain and suffering are opportunities for growth of the human spirit." They would become aware of the fact that through these limiting forces they are being redeemed by the God who is the ultimate power to whom these forces are subjected. They would then recognize that they are being refined by God rather than being destroyed.[33]

Niebuhr elaborates on this point as follows: "And there is present the polarity of the divine-human dialogue: God acts redemptively, but there is no redemption until free men respond to the divine act. Man responds to God in the exercise of his will, his created freedom; thus God can give man through his redemption a new freedom [from limitations][34] (brackets mine).

It becomes evident that God and his power are present in every action that comes down upon the South African adult and all of us. This is an action that liberates from stagnation and unresponsiveness/irresponsibility. It is also an action that redeems us from a life of negation [in South Africa] to a life of grace[35] (brackets mine). Pastoral care to blacks in South Africa with the aid of our model can be effectively used to aid them to live their lives in response to God, first, and second, fearlessly toward limiting forces in society. Then they will muster the strength to forgive those who limit them as they have been forgiven by God.[36]

Stagnation and irresponsibility in our psychosocial-religio environment should be subjected to a reinterpretation, a reinterpretation that stems from a response to God based on trust and love and not fear and limitation. This is the only adequate response that can counteract stagnation and unresponsiveness toward God. In his article, "War as the Judgment of God," Niebuhr stresses

some points which are helpful for the implication of his
ethics for pastoral care in South Africa. He wrote,
"...it is a sign of a returning health when God rather than
the self or the enemy is seen to be the central figure in the
great tragedy of war and when the question 'What must I
do?' is preceded by the question 'What is God doing?'"
      South Africa is currently in a state of civil war. If
one draws an analogy between the second world war and
South Africa, then Niebuhr's point is appropriate. Black
adults can be made generative and responsive/responsible
if through pastoral care they are aided to focus their
energies on God, rather than on "the enemy" (dominant
group), as the central figure in that tragedy. This can only
be done in faith and could help to retrieve the health that
has been lost through self-absorption caused by racism,
apartheid, etc., as well as by unresponsiveness and various
other negative psychosocial dynamics in their personalities.
      Another point of significance for the moral life of the
black South African in Niebuhr's thinking is that when this
reinterpretation has taken place these adults could be
enabled to have a more fitting response to actions upon
them. They could also have a new attitude towards these
actions, an attitude of trust and faith in the fact that God
knows what he is doing.
      A further point that Capps points out that is helpful
in informing pastoral care in South Africa is the following.
Under his subheading entitled, "Developmental Approach to
Life,"[37] he states that there is an element of the
developmental approach to life in the Wisdom Literature of
the Bible.   The Biblical approach to pastoral care and
counseling is a position that I strongly advocate. Therefore
Capps' idea in this regard is very helpful. Proverbs shares
Erikson's developmental approach to life, according to
Capps, particularly insofar as the emphasis on the social
matrix out of which the individual's growth and maturity
evolves is concerned.[38] Proverbs shows that development is
not an individual but a societal task. This latter point is

strongly stressed by Erikson, and it is one of the strong points of divergence between Freud's thinking and his. It is at this level that Erikson steers his developmental course away from the psychosexual (Freud) to the psychosocial factors that influence human development.

When viewed from the perspective of generativity and responsibility important insights come to light which could be utilized by pastors. In the same manner that generativity evolves through a number of stages, e.g., from childhood morality through contact with the parent to the adult ethical stage responsibility also evolves in a more or less developmental sense. Niebuhr did not state the evolvement of responsibility in terms of stages and may not agree with my way of interpretation. The adult's sense of responsibility also evolves and matures to higher levels as their faith in God develops and matures. My reason for referring to Niebuhr's idea of responsibility is due to an elaboration of some points that he stresses about acceptance, affirmation, understanding, and cultivation of a response of love.[39] On drawing an analogy with Erikson's stages the following comes to light:

> To "merely accept what is" is analogous to the stage of trust vs. mistrust.
>
> To "affirm oneself..." is analogous to the stage of autonomy vs. shame and doubt.
>
> The "desire to understand" is analogous to the stage of identity vs. identity confusion.
>
> Niebuhr's idea of "cultivation" in the context of response is analogous to the stage of generativity vs. stagnation.[40]

When viewed from the above perspective Niebuhr's ethics of responsibility has a developmental character.

Finally, Capps shows how Erikson's theory could provide reference points for life's journey which could be engaged by the pastor for pastoral care purposes.[41] These reference points could enable the care receiver to keep a generative-responsible perspective throughout life. Niebuhr's ethics also sketches some reference points which could be effectively employed in the rendering of pastoral care. We shall mention a few of these: "Man or Woman as Answerer," and "The Faith Triad."

Niebuhr's thoughts on Jesus as our paradigm of responsibility are of crucial importance for the understanding and effective interpretation of our response in a divine and universal context. Jesus is a rational power who stands in stark contrast to the irrational powers of stagnation that seek to limit the black adult and to take away his sense of self in South Africa. The event of his revelation to the Christian community, in South Africa in particular, enables them to place their trust in God through Jesus Christ as well as complete trust and confidence in God's actions. This in turn would restore to the Christian individual a sense of unified selfhood in Christ.[42] "The heart that reasons with the image of revelation, however, keeps discovering the possibility of the resurrection of a new and other self, of a new community, a reborn remnant."[43] We may therefore draw the conclusion that the revelation event makes possible rebirth or conversion which in turn would restore generativity and responsibility in a relationship and new connectedness with God.

This new "I" could be used in the service of God to break the closed society which South Africa is so that God's generative, responsible kingdom could be ushered in for all people in that land irrespective of race or color. This would be a community where love, justice, and righteousness can reign supreme--a new Covenant community, redeemed and renewed by God through Jesus Christ our Lord.

This revelation of Jesus Christ to the Christian community in South Africa, when translated into Loder's terms,[44] is an event of convictional knowing or a transforming experience. This experience further reinforces our ideas on responsibility and generativity in the context of pastoral care in South Africa. In his chapter, "From Negation to Love,"[45] Loder states the following:

Normal human development has a *theological deficiency*. It is constructed on a psychological-sociocultural foundation. This is why I chose Niebuhr to act as a corrective in this regard. A translation into Niebuhrian terms reveals that one crucial angle of the Faith Triad is left out of the picture in normal human development, namely God. Thus, this kind of development is restricted to just two points of the Faith Triad, that is, Self and Other Selves. Normal human development thus proceeds along the lines of an impoverished pattern. That is why Erikson, who is not a theologian but a religious person, points out the elements of ethics and the numinous so vividly. He too was aware of this theological deficiency. Our understanding of normal human development needs to be transformed. Niebuhr has already been helpful in this regard. Loder strengthens Niebuhr's position in certain ways especially with his thoughts about transformational negation.[46]

Loder mentions four general types of negation that are crucial in the process of human transformation, namely, calculative, functional, existential, and transformational. We shall only focus on the latter two.

"Existential negation may also be understood as the ultimate negation of the capacity of the ego to construct its world, sometimes called ego shock."[47] "The term transformational negation refers to the negation of negation such that a new integration emerges establishing a gain over the original negated state or condition."[48] When the double negation is brought into existence.[49] The first negation is incorporated into this "new state of being." This is the kind of being that the pastors in South Africa should bring into existence with the aid of our model. Loder says that when the existential transformation occurs there is a simultaneous occurrence of the negation of the "experience of nothingness."[50] The possibility that existed previously whereby the individual could express a state of non-being is removed.

The event of the revelation of Jesus Christ through kerygma and convictional knowing/existential transformation (Loder) established the indispensable dimension of the Biblical/Spiritual ethos of the alternate pastoral care method that we wish to employ in South Africa. It furthermore reinforces the fact that Jesus Christ is the cornerstone of the ethical dimension of this method. Through Christ the transforming process of the "black ego" is accomplished and entrusted to the Divine actions of God through faith. He is the mediator and negator of their experience of nothingness" in the context of the South African situation. This nothingness could also be referred to in terms of stagnation and irresponsibility. Loder may refer to this "Black Adult Ego Transformation" not in terms of demolition of the ego but as "decisive recentering of the personality around a transcendental reality that points to the invisible God."[51]

When this process has occurred the ego is displaced, but with positive effects. Ego functioning is now even stronger because the "ego has less need to control or limit perceptions or understandings of self, world, or others,"[52] as it is no longer the fulcrum of the personality, but God's presence and power is. This presence and this power negate the limitations on the black personality particularly those that curtail their range for ethical action.

D. *The Moral Context of Pastoral Care (Browning)*

By far the most important insight given by this book is the fact that responsibility and generativity have a moral context. Therefore, the kind of pastoral care that is given to black adults in South Africa should be governed by the fact that problems that have traditionally been labelled personal are usually linked to and have a larger ethical context.[53] Our focus on generativity and responsibility lead to the conclusion that there are strong connections between personal problems and larger ethical questions. Problems that pertain to responsibility and generativity can therefore not be treated in isolation. We must pay attention to the larger moral context out of which they evolve. If we fail to do so we could restrict those issues to the personal-emotional dimension of life and make ourselves, as pastors, guilty of perpetuating irresponsibility and ungenerativity. The large context in which modern pastoral care is located in South Africa "governs its specific goals and procedures."[54] If relevant pastoral care that will meet the needs of the ungenerative and irresponsible person is to take place in South Africa, pastors should pay serious attention to matters relating to context. What do we mean by context?

> To say that pastoral care has a context is to say that it takes place in a community known as the church with larger goals, characteristic styles, preferred means, and specifiable relations with other institutions as well as with the larger society of which it is a part.[55]

The church on the other hand is located in a larger context, that is, society. This society has an ethos and goals of its own. Browning refers to the church as a subsystem of the larger society and to pastoral care as a subsystem of the church.[56] What does this say for the pastoral care of the church in South Africa? The church in South Africa must always be aware of the connection between the care receivers who form part of its fellowship and their relationship to the society at large. This society and the parishioner have a reciprocal effect on each other. The parishioner has to deal with a secular world and the secular world has to deal with a spiritual church. As the Christian care receiver is influenced by the value symbols in society this influence will overlap with his church life.

The question arises. How does this individual, e.g., black adult in South Africa, respond to the larger society that limits his range for ethical action? We have already pointed out that the answer is irresponsibility and ungenerativity. These individuals are crying out to their pastors for ethical direction and moral guidance that is coupled to their psychological development and moral lives which are deeply affected by a stagnant society. But, do pastors hear these cries with the full implications that they carry? The answer is negative.

Browning says, "...the problem may be in the tools themselves."[57] I have already alluded to the fact that the "traditional pastoral tools" employed by pastors in South Africa have become obsolete. I want to suggest that these "tools" should be changed. The argument for the engagement of our model as a "pastoral tool" that takes into consideration a moral context is very appropriate in this regard.

Due to the fact that so many black pastors in South Africa do not pay attention to context they have become embedded in a severe identity crisis.[58] In many cases pastoral care and pastoral counseling have become mixed up.

> Pastoral care is now more readily seen as something done by ministers to help people in a situation of emotional conflict and crisis....Pastoral care has tended to focus on the important but limited functions of pastoral counseling.[59]

On the basis of this study I would recommend the following to pastors in South Africa who render pastoral care and counseling to black adults:

To Black Pastors: They should be faithful to God in the methods that they employ for pastoral care and pastoral counseling. This implies that they should not be embedded in timidity when the need arises to engage the prophetic dimension of pastoral care as Clinebell and Seifert advocate. This means that the political sphere of existence of blacks in South Africa should not be ignored. This will require great courage. But, God will empower them with the spiritual resources that are required to proceed in this fashion.

To White Pastors in Black Congregations: They should reassess their pastoral care methods by using Jesus as their norm. If their methods do not conform to his teaching, love, care, and righteousness then they should humbly reconstitute them. They should question the hierarchical structure of their allegiance in rendering pastoral care. If they discover that their prime consideration is patriotism and nationalism they should allow the Spirit to give them an awareness and a recognition of their need to repent and to restructure their pastoral care and counseling methods.

To both of the above groups I would suggest that Don Browning offers a most adequate guideline for executing pastoral care in the current South African situation. Browning's arguments about the moral context of pastoral care serve as a corrective for Hiltner's eductive methods as we have pointed out before.

> Whatever the virtues of eductive counseling as a model for pastoral care...its overemphasis signals a default on the part of the Protestant community. It is unwilling to tackle the hard problems of reconstructing the normative moral and cultural value symbols by means of which the church and its members should live.... When the spirit of eductive counseling pervades the church, the tough value issues are left up to the

individual's tastes and preferences. The church
and the minister can properly address only the
interpersonal and emotional dynamics.[60]

Browning's argument is in favor of a pastoral care
method that takes a holistic view of the problems that
people are faced with. While Hiltner's method has its
merits it is left wanting particularly in a society where
rapid social change is being experienced. Karl Menninger's
voice can also be added to Browning's argument for pastors
to pay greater attention to the moral context of care. In his
book, *Whatever Became of Sin*,[61] Menninger says that clergy
or psychiatrists do not talk about sin anymore. The
emphasis is rather on disease and treatment. This is partly
due to the fact that the church is ignoring the value symbols
of society that influence our decision-making.[62] No wonder
that the inner world of care seekers stays in a perpetual
state of crisis, fear, and tension.

Carl Rogers wrote about the struggle that people
experience in trying to become themselves.[63] In his chapter
entitled, "What it means to become a person," he says that
every normal individual has a desire to be himself/herself.
His way of assisting individuals to achieve that is by means
of his method of Client-centered Therapy.[64] Rogers says
that in order to facilitate the process of becoming the
individual must be aided to examine the mask that conceals
the true self. "He discovers how much of his life is guided
by what he thinks he should be, not by what he is."[65] When
black adults fear those who impose limitations on them
their responsibility/ responsiveness and generativity is
inhibited due to the fact that they are unable to be their
God-ordained selves. Their response of fear causes them to
be hypocritical and to wear masks so that their true
feelings, angers, resentment, and hostility may not be
detected. Rogers' method enables such individuals to
discover how much of their power is controlled by others
and how much of their limitations are self-imposed.

Together with our ethical-psychological instrument or model Rogers could also assist the black pastor in South Africa to render an effective form of pastoral care. Rogers uses the thinking of Kierkegaard to illumine the above dilemma of the individual more clearly viz. Kierkegaard states that "...the deepest form of despair is to *choose* to be another than himself."[66] Rogers says that the greatest responsibility of the individual is to choose to be one's true self.

If we could assist the black adult in South Africa to choose to be himself/herself with full awareness that there are risks involved there is a distinct possibility that their range for ethical action could be increased. They could become less fearful of the stagnant forces in their environment that they feared before, and

> The individual comes to feel that the locus of evaluation lies within himself. Less and less does he look to others for approval; for standards to live by; for decisions and choices. He recognized that it rests within himself to choose; that the only question which matters is, "Am I living in a way which is deeply satisfying to me, and which truly expresses me?" This is perhaps the most important question for the creative individual.[67]

Black South African adults are posing a major challenge to pastors and pastoral care in South Africa particularly as they grapple with the issues of responsibility and generativity in their lives. Moral guidance is needed in the South African black church more than ever before. Times are critical and the issues in question are serious. However, the black church in South Africa still has an opportunity to reconstitute her pastoral care methods in a relevant way so that she can become a more effective tool for God. There is still hope because the God whom we serve is the source of responsibility and generativity. With his help and guidance the desired transformation could take place in a very troubled land.

NOTES

Introduction

[1] H. Richard Niebuhr, *The Meaning of Revelation* (New York: The Macmillan Company, 1941) p. 93.

[2] H. Richard Niebuhr, *The Responsible Self* (New York: Harper & Row, 1963), p. 87.

[3] Ibid., p. 87.

[4] Ibid., p. 88.

[5] James Loder, *The Transforming Moment* (New York: Harper & Row, 1981).

[6] Ibid., p. 170.

[7] Ibid., p. 171.

[8] Paul Pruyser, *The Minister as Diagnostician* (Philadelphia: The Westminster Press, 1976).

[10] Don Browning, ed., *Practical Theology* (New York: Harper & Row, 1983).

[11] Don Browning, "Pastoral Theology in a Pluralistic Age" in *Practical Theology* (New York: Harper & Row, 1981), pp. 187-201.

[12] Ibid., p. 187.

[13] James Lapsley, "Practical Theology and Pastoral Care" in *Practical Theology* (New York: Harper & Row, 1983), pp. 167-185.

[14] Ibid., p. 170.

[15] Howard Clinebell and Harvey Seifert, "Interdependence of the Pastoral and the Prophetic" in *Pastoral Psychology* (November 1969), pp. 7-14.

[16] Charles Gerkin, *The Living Human Document* (Nashville: Abingdon Press, 1984), p. 39.

[17] Ibid., p. 49.

[18] Erik Erikson, *Young Man Luther* (New York: W. W. Norton & Co., 1958).

[19] H. Richard Niebuhr, *The Responsible Self* (New York: Harper & Row, 1963), p. 42.

[20] Ibid., p. 8.

[21] John Kotre, *Outliving the Self* (Baltimore: The Johns Hopkins Press, 1984).

²² Don Browning, *Religious Ethics and Pastoral Care* (Philadelphia: Fortress Press, 1983), p. 15.
²³ Peter Berger, *The Sacred Canopy* (Garden City, NY: Doubleday and Co., 1967), pp. 141-171.
²⁴ Don Browning, *Religious Ethics and Pastoral Care*, p. 15.
²⁵ Ibid., p. 16.
²⁶ Erik Erikson, *Toys and Reasons* (New York: W. W. Norton & Co., 1977), p. 89.
²⁷ Carol Gilligin, *In a Different Voice* (Cambridge, MA: Harvard University Press, 1982).
²⁸ Ibid., p. 156.

Chapter 1. Erikson's Life Cycle Theory

¹ Henry W. Maier, *Three Theories of Child Development* (New York: Harper & Row Publishers, 1965), p. 17.
² Ibid.
³ Erik Erikson, *Childhood and Society* (New York: W. W. Norton and Company, 1963), p. 12.
⁴ Maier, p. 18.
⁵ Maier, *Three Theories of Child Development*.
⁶ Ibid., p. 20.
⁷ Erikson, p. 32.
⁸ Maier, p. 22.
⁹ Ibid., p. 26.
¹⁰ Eugene Wright, *Identity and Religion* (New York: The Seabury Press, 1982), p. 38.
¹¹ Erik Erikson, *Insight and Responsibility* (New York: W. W. Norton and Company, 1964), p. 114.
¹² Donald Capps, *Life Cycle Theory and Pastoral Care* (Philadelphia: Fortress Press, 1983), p. 23.
¹³ Maier, p. 32.
¹⁴ Erikson, *Childhood and Society*, p. 270.
¹⁵ Erik Erikson, *The Life Cycle Completed* (New York: W. W. Norton and Company, 1982), p. 32.

16 Erikson, *The Life Cycle Completed*, p. 249.
17 Ibid., p. 247.
18 Erikson, *Insight and Responsibility*, p. 119.
19 Erikson, *Identity Youth and Crisis* (New York: W. W. Norton and Company, 1968), p. 96.
20 Erikson, *Identity and the Life Cycle* (New York: W. W. Norton and Company, 1980), p. 68.
21 Ibid.
22 Ibid., p. 80.
23 Paul Roazen, *Erik Erikson* (New York: The Free Press, 1976), p. 114.
24 Erikson, *Childhood and Society*, p. 259.
25 Ibid., p. 260.
26 Erikson, *Identity and the Life Cycle*, p. 90.
27 Erikson, *Childhood and Society*, p. 261.
28 Ibid., p. 263.
29 Erikson, *Identity and the Life Cycle*, p. 90.
30 Charles Kao, *Psychological and Religious Development* (Washington: University Press of America, Inc., 1981), p. 209.
31 Erikson, *Identity Youth and Crisis*, p. 132.
32 Ibid., p. 37.
33 Ibid., p. 38.
34 Ibid., p. 39.
35 Ibid., p. 20.
36 Ibid., p. 22.
37 Erik Erikson, *Young Man Luther* (New York: W. W. Norton and Co., 1960).
38 Erikson, *Identity Youth and Crisis*, p. 30.
39 Erikson, *Childhood and Society*, p. 263.
40 Erik Erikson, "Psychosocial Identity," *International Encyclopedia of Social Science*, Vol. 7, p. 63.
41 *Daedalus*, Spring 1976.
42 Ibid.
43 Erikson, *Childhood and Society*, p. 264.
44 Ibid.
45 Ibid., p. 267.

[46] Erikson, *Identity and the Life Cycle*, p. 103.
[47] Ibid., p. 71.
[48] Ibid., p. 72.
[49] Don Browning, *Generative Man*, p. 145.
[50] Erikson, *Identity and the Life Cycle*, p. 105.
[51] Browning, *Generative Man*, p. 47.
[52] Erik Erikson, *Gandhi's Truth* (New York: W. W. Norton and Co., 1969), p. 132.
[53] Erikson, *Insight and Responsibility*, p. 228.
[54] Browning, *Generative Man*, p. 160.
[55] Ibid., p. 162.
[56] Ibid., p. 164.
[57] Martin Buber, *I and Thou* (New York: Charles Scribner, 1970).
[58] Browning, *Generative Man*, p. 153.
[59] John Kotre, *Outliving the Self* (Baltimore: The Johns Hopkins University Press, 1984), p. 10.
[60] Ibid., p. 11.
[61] Ibid., p. 14.
[62] Ibid., p. 16.
[63] Erikson, *Insight and Responsibility*, p. 113.
[64] Ibid., p. 114.
[65] Ibid., p. 118.
[66] Ibid., p. 119.
[67] Ibid., p. 122.
[68] Ibid., p. 124.
[69] Ibid., p. 129.
[70] Ibid., p. 131.
[71] Ibid., p. 131.
[72] Ibid., p. 133.
[73] Erikson, *Identity, Youth and Crisis*, p. 92.
[74] Wright, *Identity and Religion*, p. 180.
[75] Ibid., p. 97.
[76] Ibid., p. 97.

Chapter 2. H. Richard Niebuhr's Ethics of Responsibility

¹ This book focuses on the Ethics of Responsibility of H. Richard Niebuhr but it is of interest to note that the backdrops of the theologies of Niebuhr and Edwards have some resemblances, e.g., both Niebuhr and Edwards did not live in a complacent age, but during periods of great change. These were periods of rationalizations. In the case of Niebuhr for example there was rationalization about race, cf. Nazism. Niebuhr lived during the aftermath of World War II, McCarthyism, the rise of Russia as a major power, the Great Depression, and during the emergence of the Eastern Bloc and the Third World. Edwards' period was one of great upheavals too. The backdrops of the theologies of these men in turn are in harmony with the period of upheaval and quest for social change by the oppressed masses in South Africa.

² Libertus Hoedemaker, *The Theology of H. Richard Niebuhr* (New York: The Pilgrim Press, 1970).

³ H. Richard Niebuhr, *The Kingdom of God in America* (New York: Harper & Row, 1937).

⁴ Hoedemaker, *The Theology of H. Richard Niebuhr*, p. 38.

⁵ Ibid., p. 45.

⁶ H. Richard Niebuhr in collaboration with Dan D. Williamson and James Gustafson, *The Purpose of the Church and its Ministry*.

⁷ H. Richard Niebuhr, *The Responsible Self* (New York: Harper & Row, 1963).

⁸ Ibid., p. 8.

⁹ Ibid., p. 14.

¹⁰ Ibid., p. 48.

¹¹ Ibid., p. 48.

¹² William K. Frankena, *Ethics* (Englewood Cliffs: Prentice Hall, 1963).

¹³ Niebuhr, *The Responsible Self*, p. 52.

¹⁴ Ibid., p. 53.

¹⁵ Ibid., p. 60.

[16] Ibid., p. 56.

[17] Ibid., p. 61.

[18] Ibid., p. 64.

[19] Jerry Irish, *The Religious Thought of H. R. Niebuhr* (Atlanta: John Knox Press, 1983).

[20] Niebuhr, *The Responsible Self*, p. 65.

[21] Irish, *The Religious Thought of H. R. Niebuhr*, p. 20.

[22] Niebuhr, *The Responsible Self*, p. 66.

[23] Ibid., p. 67.

[24] Ibid., p. 67.

[25] A. S. Knight, "Responsibility and Obligation in the Ethics of H. R. Niebuhr," Microfilm No. 1419.

[26] H. R. Niebuhr, *The Responsible Self*, p. 72.

[27] Paul E. Pfuetze, *The Social Self* (New York: Bookman Associates, 1954), p. 83.

[28] Ibid.

[29] Robert Keagan, *The Evolving Self* (Cambridge: Harvard University Press), p. 29.

[30] H. R. Niebuhr, *The Social Self*, p. 79.

[31] Ibid., pp. 154-155.

[32] "Psychology of Social Consciousness Implied in Instruction," *Science* XXXI (1910):691-92.

[33] H. R. Niebuhr, *The Social Self*, p. 230.

[34] Ibid., p. 232.

[35] Hoedemaker, *The Theology of H. Richard Niebuhr*, p. 67.

[36] H. Richard Niebuhr, *Christ and Culture* (New York: Harper & Row), pp. 243-246.

[37] H. R. Niebuhr, *The Responsible Self*, p. 97.

[38] Hoedemaker, *The Theology of H. Richard Niebuhr*, p. 77.

[39] H. R. Niebuhr, *The Responsible Self*, p. 79.

[40] H. Richard Niebuhr, *The Meaning of Revelation*, p. 80.

[41] H. Richard Niebuhr, "The Triad of Faith," *Andover Newton Bulletin* XLVII (October 1954):3-12.

[42] H. Richard Niebuhr, *Radical Monotheism and Western Culture* (New York: Harper & Row, 1943), pp. 100-113.

[43] Ibid., p. 100.

[44] Ibid., p. 100.

45 Ibid., p. 103.
46 Ibid., p. 107.
47 Ibid., p. 109.
48 Ibid., p. 110.
49 Ibid., p. 112.
50 Hoedemaker, *The Theology of H. R. Niebuhr*, p. 70.
51 Ibid., p. 50.
52 H. R. Niebuhr, *Radical Monotheism and Western Culture* (New YOrk: Harper & Row, 1943), p. 100.
53 Ibid., p. 105.
54 H. R. Niebuhr, *Radical Monotheism and Western Culture*.
55 Hoedemaker, *The Theology of H. Richard Niebuhr*, p. 91.
56 H. R. Niebuhr, *Radical Monotheism and Western Culture*, p. 11.
57 Ibid., p. 16.
58 Ibid., p. 16.
59 Ibid., p. 24.
60 Ibid., p. 32.
61 Ibid., p. 32.
62 Ibid., p. 34.
63 H. R. Niebuhr, *The Purpose of the Church and Its Ministry*.
64 Ibid., p. 64.
65 Waldo Beach, *The Christian Life* (Richmond: The C.L.C. Press, 1966), pp. 66-67.
66 Ibid., p. 67.
67 Ibid., p. 67.
68 Ibid., p. 154.
69 H. R. Niebuhr, *The Responsible Self,* p. 158.
70 Ibid.
71 Ibid., p. 165.
72 Ibid., p. 166.
73 Hoedemaker, *The Theology of H. Richard Niebuhr*, pp. 158-159.
74 James Fowler, *To See the Kingdom* (Nashville: Abingdon Press, 1974), p. 26.

⁷⁵ E. Clinton Gardner, "Responsibility and Moral Direction in the Ethics of H. Richard Niebuhr," *Encounter* 40 (Spring 1977):143-68.
⁷⁶ Ibid., p. 145.
⁷⁷ H. R. Niebuhr, *The Responsible Self*, p. 12.
⁷⁸ Ibid., p. 16.
⁷⁹ H. Richard Niebuhr, *The Meaning of Revelation* (New York: The Macmillan Company, 1941), p. 43.
⁸⁰ Ibid., p. 60.
⁸¹ Ibid., p. 70.
⁸² Ibid., p. 72.
⁸³ Ibid., p. 81.
⁸⁴ Ibid., p. 87.
⁸⁵ Ibid., p. 87.
⁸⁶ Ibid., p. 93.
⁸⁷ Ibid., p. 109.
⁸⁸ Ibid., p. 116.
⁸⁹ Ibid., p. 138.
⁹⁰ Ibid., p. 153.
⁹¹ Waldo Beach, *Christian Ethics*.
⁹² H. Richard Niebuhr, *The Responsible Self*, p. 144.
⁹³ Ibid., p. 136.

Chapter 3. An Ethical-Psychological Model

¹ Ian Ramsey, *Models and Mystery* (London: Oxford University Press, 1962).
² Max Black, *Models and Metaphors* (New York: Cornel University Press, 1962).
³ Ibid., p. 122.
⁴ Ramsey, p. 2.
⁵ Ibid., p. 7.
⁶ Ibid., p. 9.
⁷ Black, p. 222.
⁸ Ibid.
⁹ Ibid., p. 223.

[10] Ibid., p. 11.
[11] Ibid., p. 11.
[12] Ibid., p. 11.
[13] Ibid., p. 14.
[14] Ibid., p. 16.
[15] Heije Faber, *Psychology of Religion* (Philadelphia: The Westminster Press, 1975).
[16] Erik Erikson, *Young Man Luther* (New York: Norton & Co., Inc., 1958).
[17] Leland Elhard, "Living Faith: Some Contributions of the Concept of Ego-Identity to the Understanding of Faith," in Peter Homans (ed.), *The Dialogue Between Psychology and Theology* (Chicago: The University of Chicago Press, 1968).
[18] Erikson, *Young Man Luther.*
[19] Elhard, p. 136.
[20] Ibid.
[21] Paul Tillich, *Dynamics of Faith* (New York: Harper & Brothers, 1957).
[22] Leland Elhard, "Living Faith: Some Contributions of the Concept of Ego-Identity to the Understanding of Faith," p. 150, quoting Soren Kierkegaard, *The Sickness Unto Death* (Princeton: Princeton University Press, 1941).
[23] Ibid., p. 151.
[24] Libertus Hoedemaker, *The Theology of H. Richard Niebuhr* (New York: The Pilgrim Press, 1970), quoting Jonathan Edwards, "The Freedom of the Will," in Perry Miller (ed.), *The Works of Jonathan Edwards* (New Haven: Yale University Press, 1957), p. 172.
[25] Elhard, p. 153.
[26] H. R. Niebuhr, *The Meaning of Revelation* (New York: The Macmillan Company, 1941).
[27] Elhard, p. 161.
[28] Ibid.
[29] Eugene Wright, *Erikson: Identity and Religion* (New York: The Seabury Press, 1982).
[30] Erik Erikson, "Reflections on the Dissent of Contemporary Youth," *Daedalus* 99 (Winter 1970), p. 167.

[31] Erikson, *Young Man Luther*; Erik Erikson, *Gandhi's Truth* (New York: W. W. Norton & Co., 1969).
[32] Erikson, *Young Man Luther*, pp. 73-74.
[33] Ibid., p. 257.
[34] Ibid., p. 201.
[35]Daniel Levinson, *Seasons of a Man's Life* (New York: Ballantine Books, 1978).
[36] Erikson, *Young Man Luther*, p. 165.
[37] Ibid., p. 166.
[38] Erik Erikson, *Insight and Responsibility* (New York: W. W. Norton & Company, Inc., 1964), p. 44.
[39] Wright, *Erikson: Identity and Religion*, p. 123.
[40] Erikson, *Young Man Luther*, p. 68.
[41] William Meisner, "Faith and Identity," in Roger Johnson (ed.) *Psychohistory and Religion* (Philadelphia: Fortress Press, 1977).
[42] Ibid., p. 103.
[43] Erikson, *Young Man Luther*, p. 70.
[44] Meisner, p. 105.
[45] Erik Erikson, *Identity and the Life Cycle* (New York: W. W. Norton & Company), p. 31.
[46] Meisner, p. 104.
[47] Erikson, *Young Man Luther*, p. 68.
[48] Meisner, p. 168.
[49] Ibid., p. 98.
[50] Hoedemaker, *The Theology of H. Richard Niebuhr*, p. 57.
[51] Meisner, p. 114.
[52] Erikson, *Young Man Luther*, pp. 213-214.
[53] Ibid., p. 58.
[54] Ibid., p. 47.
[55] Ibid., p. 213.
[56] Kenneth Cauthen, "An Introduction to the Theology of H. Richard Niebuhr," *Canadian Journal of Theology* 10:4-14 (January 1964), pp. 4-14.
[57] H. Richard Niebuhr, *The Responsible Self* (New York: Harper & Row, 1963), p. 71.
[58] Ibid., p. 86.

[59] Ibid., p. 103.

[60] E. Clinton Gardner, "Responsibility and Moral Direction in the Ethics of H. Richard Niebuhr," *Encounter* (Spring 1977), pp. 143-164.

[61] Richard Niebuhr, "The Responsibility of the Church for Society." In K. S. Latourette (ed.), *The Gospel, the Church, and the World* (New York: Harper & Brothers, 1946), pp. 111-133.

[62] Ibid.

[63] H. Richard Niebuhr, *The Responsible Self,* p. 123.

[64] Thomas T. McFaul, "Dilemmas in H. Richard Niebuhr's Ethics," *Journal of Religion* 54:35-50 (January 1974), pp. 35-50.

[65] Ibid., p. 36.

[66] Eugene Wright, *Erikson: Identity and Religion.* p. 61.

[67] Erikson, *Identity Youth and Crisis,* p. 208.

[68] Ibid., p. 209.

[69] Ibid., p. 211.

[70] Ibid., p. 211.

[71] Ibid., p. 211.

[72] Ibid., p. 211

[73] Ibid., p. 217.

[74] Ibid., p. 211.

[75] H. Richard Niebuhr, *The Responsible Self,* p. 119.

[76] Ibid.

[77] Ibid., p. 123.

[78] Ibid., p. 123.

[79] Ibid., p. 101.

[80] Ibid., p. 102.

[81] Hoedemaker, *The Theology of H. R. Niebuhr,* p. 67.

[82] Ibid., p. 68.

[83] Peter Homans (ed.), *The Dialogue Between Psychology and Theology* (Chicago: The University of Chicago Press), p. 62.

[84] Ibid., p. 63.

[85] Reinhold Niebuhr, *The Self and the Dramas of History* (New York: Charles Scribner's and Sons, 1955), pp.. 127-144.

[86] H. Richard Niebuhr, *The Responsible Self,* p. 118.
[87] Ibid.
[88] Ibid.
[89] Ibid., p. 123.
[90] Erik Erikson, *Toys and Reasons* (New York: W. W. Norton and Co., 1977), p. 90.
[91] Ibid.
[92] H. Richard Niebuhr, *Radical Monotheism and Western Culture* (New York:
Harper & Row, 1943), p. 64.
[93] Erik Erikson, *Childhood and Society,* p. 262.
[94] Ibid.

Chapter 4. The Stories of Five Adults - Case Studies

[1] Donald Capps, *Pastoral Care: A Thematic Approach* (Philadelphia: The Westminster Press, 1979).
[2] Ibid., p. 15.
[3] Ibid., p. 47.
[4] Ibid., p. 47.
[5] John Kotre, *Outliving the Self* (London: The Johns Hopkins University Press, 1984), pp. 29-36.
[6] H. Richard Niebuhr, *The Responsible Self.*
[7] Ibid., p. 63.
[8] Ibid., pp. 63-64.
[9] Erik Erikson, *Childhood and Society* (New York: W. W. Norton & Co., Inc., 1963), p. 259.
[10] Erik Erikson, *Identity Youth and Crisis,* p. 259.
[11] Jerry Irish, *The Religious Thought of H. Richard Niebuhr* (Atlanta: John Knox Press, 1983), p. 19.
[12] Ibid., p. 15.
[13] Robert Coles, *Erik H. Erikson: The Growth of His Work* (Boston: Little, Brown and Company, 1970), p. 138.
[14] Ibid., p. 354.

Chapter 5. Implications for Pastoral Care in South Africa

[1] Donald Capps, *Life Cycle Theory and Pastoral Care* (Philadelphia: Fortress Press, 1983).

[2] Don Browning, *The Moral Context of Pastoral Care* (Philadelphia: The Westminster Press, 1976).

[3] Anton Boison, *The Exploration of the Inner World* (Philadelphia: University of Pennsylvania Press, 1936), p. 11.

[4] Charles Gerkin, *The Living Human Document* (Nashville: Abingdon Press, 1984), p. 39.

[5] Richard Palmer, *Hermeneutics* (Evanston: Northwestern University Press, 1969), p. 98.

[6] Charles Gerkin, *The Living Human Document*, p. 41.

[7] Edward J. Barnes, "The Black Community as the Source of Positive Self-Concept for Black Children: A Theoretical Perspective," in *Black Psychology* (New York: Harper & Row, 1980), p. 114.

[8] Erving Goffman, *Stigma* (Englewood Cliffs, NJ: Prentice Hall, Inc., 1963), p. 5.

[9] Erik Erikson, *Childhood and Society* (W. W. Norton and Company, Inc., 1963), p. 5.

[10] Erving Goffman, *Stigma*, p. 5.

[11] Charles Gerkin, *The Living Human Document*, p. 40.

[12] Ibid., p. 40.

[13] Ibid., p. 43.

[14] Ibid., p. 44.

[15] Ibid., p. 44.

[16] Hans-George Gadamer, *Truth and Method* (New York: The Seabury Press, 1975), pp. 269-274.

[17] Charles Gerkin, *The Living Human Document*, p. 44.

[18] Hans-George Gadamer, *Truth and Method* (New York: The Seabury Press, 1975), p. 273.

[19] Ibid., p. 47.

[20] Seward Hiltner, *Preface to Pastoral Theology* (Nashville: Abingdon Press, 1958), p. 151.

[21] Charles Gerkin, *The Living Human Document*, pp. 45-46.

[22] Capps, *Life Cycle Theory and Pastoral Care,* pp. 17-53.
[23] Ibid., p. 20.
[24] Ibid., p. 20.
[25] Ibid., p. 24.
[26] Ibid., p. 34.
[27] Ibid., p. 34.
[28] Erik Erikson, *The Life Cycle Completed* (New York: W. W. Norton & Co., 1982), p. 69.
[29] Capps, *Life Cycle Theory and Pastoral Care,* p. 39.
[30] Ibid., p. 40.
[31] Ibid., p. 40.
[32] H. Richard Niebuhr, *The Responsible Self,* p. 162.
[33] Ibid., p. 36.
[34] Ibid., p. 38.
[35] Ibid., p. 39.
[36] Ibid., p. 40.
[37] Donald Capps, *Life Cycle Theory and Pastoral Care,* p. 103.
[38] Ibid.
[39] H. Richard Niebuhr, *The Responsible Self,* p. 31.
[40] Ibid.
[41] Donald Capps, *Life Cycle Theory and Pastoral Care,* p. 117.
[42] Libertus Hoedemaker, *The Theology of H. Richard Niebuhr,* p. 101.
[43] Ibid.
[44] James Loder, *The Transforming Moment* (New York: Harper & Row, 1981).
[45] Ibid., pp. 161-182.
[46] Ibid., pp. 162-164, 186-187.
[47] Ibid., p. 163.
[48] Ibid., p. 163.
[49] Ibid., p. 163.
[50] Ibid., p. 164.
[51] Ibid.., p. 170.
[52] Ibid., p. 171.
[53] Don Browning, *The Moral Context of Pastoral Care,* p. 16.

[54] Ibid., p. 17.
[55] Ibid., p. 18.
[56] Ibid., p. 19.
[57] Ibid., p. 22.
[58] Ibid., p. 23.
[59] Ibid., p. 21.
[60] Ibid., p. 25.
[61] Karl Menninger, *Whatever Became of Sin* (New York: Hawthorne Books, 1973).
[62] Don Browning, *The Moral Context of Pastoral Care*, p. 25.
[63] Carl Rogers, *On Becoming a Person* (Boston: Houghton Mifflin Company, 1961).
[64] Ibid., pp. 243-269.
[65] Ibid., p. 110.
[66] Ibid., p. 110.
[67] Ibid., p. 119.

REFERENCES

Allport, Gordon. *The Nature of Prejudice*. Massachusetts: Addison-Wesley Publishing Co., 1954.

Barnes, Edward J. "The Black Community as the Source of Positive Self-Con-cept for Black Children: A Theoretical Perspective." In *Black Psyclology*. New York: Harper & Row, 1980.

Beach, Waldo. *The Christian Life*. Garden City, NY: Doubleday and Co., 1967.

Berger, Peter. *The Sacred Canopy*. New York: Harper & Row, 1983.

Black, Max. *Models and Metaphors*. New York: Cornell University Press, 1962.

Boison, Anton. *The Exploration of the Inner World*. Philadelphia: The University of Pennsylvania Press, 1936.

Broad, C. D. *Five Types of Ethical Theory*. London: Harcourt, Brace & Co., 1930.

Browning, Don. *Generative Man*. Philadelphia: The Westminster Press, 1973.

_____. "Pastoral Theology in a Pluralistic Age." *In Practical Theology*. New York: Harper & Row, 1981.

_____. *Practical Theology*. New York: Harper & Row, 1983.

_____. *The Moral Context of Pastoral Care*. Philadelphia: The Westminster Press, 1976.

230   *Pastoral Care to Black South Africans*

_____. *Religious Ethics and Pastoral Care.* Philadelphia: Fortress Press, 1983.

Buber, Martin. *I and Thou.* New York: Charles Scribner, 1970.

Capps, Donald. *Life Cycle Theory and Pastoral Care.* Philadelphia: Fortress Press, 1983.

_____. *Pastoral Care: A Thematic Approach.* Philadelphia: The Westminster Press, 1979.

Cauthen, Kenneth. "An Introduction to the Theology of H. Richard Niebuhr," *Canadian Journal of Theology* 10:4-14 (January 1964).

Clinebell, Howard and Harvey Seifert. "Interdependence of the Pastoral and the Prophetic," in *Pastoral Psychology* (November 1969)

Coles, Robert. *Erik H. Erikson: The Growth of His Work.* Boston: Little Brown and Company, 1970.

Daedalus (Spring 1976).

Dunne, John. *A Search for God in Time and Memory.* Indiana: University of Notre Dame Press, 1967.

Elhard, Leland. "Living Faith: Some Contributions of the Concept of Ego-Identity to the Understanding of Faith." In Peter Homans (ed.). *The Dialogue Between Psychology and Theology.* Chicago: The University of Chicago Press, 1968.

Erikson, Erik. *Childhood and Society.* New York: W. W. Norton & Co., 1963.

_____. *Dimensions of a New Identity.* New York: W. W. Norton & Co., 1974.

_____. *Gandhi's Truth.* New York: W. W. Norton & Co., 1969.

_____. *Identity and the Life Cycle.* New York: W. W. Norton & Co., 1980.

_____. *Identity Youth and Crisis.* New York: W. W. Norton & Co., 1968.

_____. *Insight and Responsibility.* New York: W. W. Norton & Co., 1964.

_____. *The Life Cycle Completed.* New York: W. W. Norton & Co., 1982.

_____. *Life History and the Historical Moment.* New York: W. W. Norton & Co., 1975.

_____. "Psychosocial Identity," in *International Encyclopedia of Social Science,* Vol. 7.

_____. "Reflections on the Dissent of Contemporary Youth." in *Daedalus* 99 (Winter 1970).

_____. *Toys and Reasons.* New York: W. W. Norton & Co., 1977.

_____. *Young Man Luther.* New York: W. W. Norton & Co., 1958.

Faber, Heije. *Psychology of Religion.* Philadelphia: The Westminster Press, 1975.

Fowler, James. *To See the Kingdom.* Nashville: Abingdon Press, 1974.

_____. *Stages of Faith.* New York: Harper & Row, 1981.

Frankena, William K. *Ethics.* Englewood Cliffs: Prentice Hall, 1963.

Frankl, Victor. *Man's Search for Meaning, An Introduction to Logotherapy.* New York: Simon and Schuster, 1959.

Freud, Sigmund. *A General Introduction to Psychoanalysis.* Horace Liveright, 1920.

Gadamer, Hans-George. *Truth and Method.* New York: The Seabury Press, 1975.

Gardner, E. Clinton. "Responsibility and Moral Direction in the Ethics of H. Richard Niebuhr," in *Encounter* 40 (Spring 1977).

Gerkin, Charles. *Crisis Experience in Modern Life.* Nashville: Abingdon Press, 1979.

_____. *The Living Human Document.* Nashville: Abingdon Press, 1984.

Goffman, Erving. *Stigma.* Englewood Cliffs, NJ: Prentice-Hall Inc. 1963.

Gustafson, James. *Christ and the Moral Life.* Chicago: University of Chicago Press, 1968.

_____. and James Laney (editors). *On Being Responsible.* New York: Harper & Row, 1968.

Hauerwas, Stanley. *Character in Christian Life: A Study in Theological Ethics.* San Antonio: Trinity University Press, 1975.

Hiltner, Seward. *Preface to Pastoral Theology.* Nashville: Abington Press, 1958.

_____. *Theological Dynamics.* Nashville: Abingdon Press, 1972.

Hoedemaker, Libertus. *The Theology of H. Richard Niebuhr.* New York: The Pilgrim Press, 1970.

Homans, Peter (ed.). *The Dialogue Between Psychology and Theology.* Chicago: The University of Chicago Press, 1968.

_____. *Theology After Freud.* New York: The Bobbs-Merrill Company, Inc., 1970.

Irish, Jerry. *The Religious Thought of H. Richard Niebuhr.* Atlanta: John Knox Press, 1983.

Jones, Reginald. *Black Psychology 2nd ed.* New York: Harper & Row Publishers, 1980.

Jung, Carl. *Man and His Symbols.* New York: Dell Publishing Company, 1964.

Johnson, Roger (ed.). *Psychohistory and Religion.* Philadelphia: Fortress Press, 1977.

Kao, Charles. *Psychological and Religious Development.* Washington: University Press of America, Inc., 1981.

Keagan, Robert. *The Evolving Self.* Cambridge: Harvard University Press, 1982.

Kelsey, Morton. *Prophetic Ministry, The Psychology and Spirituality of Pastoral Care.* New York: Crossroad, 1984.

Kepnes, Steven, and David Tracy. *The Challenge of Psychology to Faith.* New York: The Seabury Press, 1982.

Kierkegaard, Soren. *The Sickness unto Death.* Princeton: Princeton University Press, 1941.

Knight, A. S. "Responsibility and Obligation in the Ethics of H. R. Niebuhr," Microfilm No. 1419.

Kohut, Heinz. *The Restoration of the Self.* Baltimore: The Johns Hopkins Press, 1984.

Kotre, John. *Outliving the Self.* Baltimore: The Johns Hopkins Press, 1984.

Lapsley, James. "Practical Theology and Pastoral Care." In *Practical Theology.* New York: Harper & Row, 1981.

Latourette, K. S. (ed.). *The Gospel, the Church, and the World.* New York: Harper & Brothers, 1946.

Levinson, Daniel. *Seasons of a Man's Life.* New York: Ballantine Books, 1978.

Lifton, Robert. *The Broken Connection.* New York: Basic Books, Inc., 1979.

Loder, James. *The Transforming Moment.* New York: Harper & Row, 1981.

McFaul, Thomas. "Dilemmas in H. Richard Niebuhr's Ethics," in *Journal of Religion* 54:35-50 (January 1974).

Maier, Henry W. *Three Theories of Child Development.* New York: Harper & Row Publishers, 1965.

May, Rollo. *Man's Search for Himself.* New York: Dell Publishing Co., 1953.

Meisner, William. "Faith and Identity." In Roger Johnson (ed.), *Psychohistory and Religion.* Philadelphia: Fortress Press, 1977.

Menninger, Karl. *Whatever Became of Sin.* New York: Hawthorne Books, 1951.

Niebuhr, H. Richard. *Christ and Culture.* New York: Harper & Row, 1951.

_____. *The Kingdom of God in America.* New York: Harper & Row, 1937.

_____. *The Meaning of Revelation.* New York: The Macmillan Co., 1941.

_____ in collaboration with Dan D. Williamson and James Gustafson. *The Purpose of the Church and its Ministry.* New York: Harper & Row, 1956.

_____. *Radical Monotheism and Western Culture.* New York: Harper & Row, 1943.

_____. *The Responsible Self.* New York: Harper & Row, 1963.

_____. "The Triad of Faith," *Andover Newton Bulletin* XLVII (October 154):3-12.

Niebuhr, Richard. "The Responsibility of the Church for Society." In K. S. Latourette (ed.), *The Gospel, the Church, and the World.* New York: Harper & Brothers, 1946.

Niebuhr, Reinhold. *The Self and the Dramas of History.* New York: Charles Scribners and Sons, 1955.

Oates, Wayne E. *An Introduction to Pastoral Counseling.* Nashville: Broadman Press, 1959.

_____. *The Psychology of Religion.* Texas: Word Books, 1973.

Oglesby, William B., Jr. *Biblical Themes for Pastoral Care.* Nashville: Abingdon, 1980.

Otto, Rudolph. *The Idea of the Holy.* New York: Oxford University Press, 1923.

Palmer, Richard. *Hermeneutics.* Evanston: Northwestern University Press, 1969.

Pfuetze, Paul E. *The Social Self.* New York: Bookman Associates, 1954.

Pruyser, Paul. *The Minister as Diagnostician.* Philadelphia: The Westminster Press, 1976.

_____. "Psychology of Social Consciousness Implied in Instruction," *Science* XXXI (1910):691-92.

Ramsey, Ian. *Models and Mystery.* London: Oxford University Press, 1962.

Roazen, Paul. *Erik Erikson.* New York: The Free Press, 1976.

Rogers, Carl. *Client-Centered Therapy.* Boston: Houghton Mifflin Company, 1965.

_____. *On Becoming a Person.* Boston: Houghton Mifflin Company, 1961.

Szasz, Thomas S. *The Myth of Mental Illness (rev. ed.).* New York: Harper & Row Publishers, 1974.

Tillich, Paul. *Dynamics of Faith.* New York: Harper & Brothers, 1957.

White, Robert. *Lives in Progress.* New York: Holt, Rinhart and Winston, 1966.

Winter, Gibson. *Liberating Creation, Foundations of Religious Social Ethics.* New York: Crossroad, 1981.

Wright, Eugene. *Identity and Religion.* New York: The Seabury Press, 1982.